COWGIRLS

Candace Savage

Ten Speed Press
Berkeley, California

For Marilyn

Ten Speed Press
Post Office Box 7123
Berkeley, California 94707

Back cover photograph: Photofest NY
Book design by Tom Brown and Barbara Hodgson

LIBRARY OF CONGRESS CATALOGING-IN-PUBLICATION DATA

Savage, Candace, 1949–
       Cowgirls / Candace Savage.
             p.   cm.
       Includes bibliographical references and index.
       ISBN 0-89815-830-3
       1. Cowgirls—West (U.S.) 2. Cowgirls—Canada, Western. 3. West
(U.S.)—Social life and customs. 4. Canada, Western—Social life
and customs. I. Title.
       F596.S234   1996
       978—dc20   96-2059
                                             CIP

Originally published by Greystone Books, a division of Douglas & McIntyre Ltd.
First Ten Speed Press printing, 1996

Printed in Hong Kong through Mandarin Offset
1 2 3 4 5 6 7 8 9 10— 00 99 98 97 96

PREVIOUS PAGES. Wild West cowgirl May Lillie was featured in two very different promotional images, both of which date from around 1900. *Buffalo Bill Historical Center, Cody, Wyoming*

CONTENTS

PREFACE

When I was a little girl, in the mid-1950s, I wanted more than anything to be a cowgirl. It wasn't until quite recently that this ambition struck me as strange. A cowgirl? There wasn't a cow within miles of my place. I lived in the city, and the field across the street was not a pasture but an airport runway. As for horses, the wooden steeds on a merry-go-round were wild enough for me. And yet, in my happiest moments, I was queen of the open range.

Being a cowgirl was a lot more fun than being a little lady, which was what my parents seemed to want of me. Little ladies wore white gloves to church and had tea parties with their dolls. They were clean and quiet and never scuffed their patent-leather toes. But cowgirls dressed in shirts and jeans and ran around with the boys. They shot cap guns and yelled and made all kinds of noise. "Bang! Bang! I got you. You're dead." "No, I'm not. You missed." That was the life!

The women in my neighborhood were full-time mothers and wives, and I knew that someday I was supposed to become one of them. But being a grown-up lady didn't look like much fun either. I decided I'd be a cowgirl instead and play the same game as the boys. It was my first impulse towards what would later become known as gender "liberation."

Fact was, if I could have managed it, I would have liked to be a cow*boy*. I was not sorry to be female, but I could see that being male had certain advantages. There was, for example, the question of holsters and guns. All the boys in the neighborhood had their own, but my parents wouldn't let me have any; they said firearms were not toys. Would they have enforced this rule, I wondered darkly, if they had had a son? It was clear to me that I had no guns of my own because

My sister Marilyn and I demonstrated our quick draws in this family vacation photo, taken about 1956. *Harry and Edna Sherk*

FACING PAGE. Calm, cool and collected, a hard-riding cowgirl galloped across a movie poster from the early years of the century. *Buffalo Bill Historical Center, Cody, Wyoming.*

I was a girl. It wasn't fair. Just like it wasn't fair that Roy Rogers hogged most of the action on TV, and Dale Evans hardly got to do anything. Nobody ever sent Roy Rogers to the café for sandwiches.

Playing cowgirl was just a kids' game but it was far from trivial. It introduced me to both the attractions and the difficulties of being female in a man's world. The cowgirl set me on the trail to becoming a feminist, and perhaps she led many other girls along the same promising path. For I was not alone in my western fantasies. There were thousands of young cowgirls, decked out in Stetsons and vests, tearing across the neatly trimmed lawns of fifties' subdivisions. Twenty years later, these same women poured out of their homes again to put their passion and energy into building the women's movement. Had playing cowgirl been a first step in shaping this vision?

When this idea occurred to me, it put the cowgirl in an entirely new focus. Suddenly, I wanted to know more about her origins and her significance. Where had she come from, with her western charm and drive? How did she establish herself in the public eye? Had she struggled for attention and respect? How did she manage to be there for us, in the fifties, just when we needed her? And finally I wondered what had become of her in recent years. Is our cowgirl hero still out there somewhere, riding the gender frontier? This book is my attempt to answer these questions.

❦

My research has led me on a long and delightful quest through libraries and archives on three continents. In particular, I would like to acknowledge the assistance of the American Heritage Center at the University of Wyoming; the British Film Institute in London; the Buffalo Bill Historical Center in Cody, Wyoming (especially Elizabeth Holmes and Lillian Turner); the Western History Collection of the Denver Public Library; the Glenbow–Alberta Institute in Calgary; the Montana Historical Society in Helena; the National Archives of Canada in Ottawa; the National Cowgirl Hall of Fame in Fort Worth, Texas (especially Virginia Artho and Danielle

Routhier); the National Fairground Archives at the University of Sheffield in England (especially Vanessa Toulmin); the National Library of Australia in Canberra; the Provincial Archives of Alberta in Edmonton; the Provincial Archives of Saskatchewan in Regina; the Umatilla Historical Society in Pendleton, Oregon; the Saskatoon Public Library and the University of Saskatchewan in Saskatoon; and the Wyoming State Museum in Cheyenne.

I am also indebted to Pat Studdy-Clift for telling me the story of her lady bushranger and to Peter N. Poole for sharing his knowledge of the history of women in Australian rodeo. Historian Mary Lou LeCompte, rodeo champion Jonnie Jonckowski, singer Patsy Montana, ranch foreman Delores Noreen, and three Saskatchewan ranchers and poets—Doris Bircham, Harvey Mawson and Thelma Poirier—all generously answered my many questions. Eminent western historian Glenda Riley kindly sent me an advance copy of her paper on Annie Oakley, critic Jack Shadoian loaned me his cowgirl comics, cowgirl poet Buzzy Vick gave me access to her western sheet music, musician Liz Masterson shared her photo of the Girls of the Golden West, and antique dealer Mary Schmitt opened her collection to me. Diana Savage proved herself an organized and efficient research assistant.

Lillian Turner of the Buffalo Bill Historical Center and Shelley Tanaka, editor in excelsis, both reviewed the manuscript for this book and made helpful suggestions for its improvement. Finally, it is a special pleasure to acknowledge the contribution of art historian Keith Bell, who not only reviewed the text and located several wonderful images for my collection, but who also shared my enthusiasm for this project through its long genesis.

An urban cowgirl reined in her tricycle long enough to pose for this portrait, circa 1954. *Shelley Tanaka*

OVERLEAF. A big-haired, bright-eyed "cowboy girl" beamed out from the cover of "The Girl I Loved Out in the Golden West," a romantic ballad that was published in Denver in 1905. *Denver Public Library, Western History Department*

THE GIRL I LOVED OUT IN THE GOLDEN WEST

TRADE MARK REG. 5, 4 D. COPYRIGHT 1905 BY CHICAGO & ALTON RAILWAY CO

COWBOY GIRL

POEM BY
C.H. SCOGGINS

MUSIC BY
CHARLES AVRIL

PUBLISHED BY THE TOLBERT R INGRAM MUSIC CO DENVER COL

REAL COWBOY GIRLS

This is a deuced fast place.

Most independent women here I ever seen.

Letter from Mollie to her friend Ann, Oregon, 1871

There are those who will tell you that the cowgirl is pure myth, just a rootin'-tootin' creation of American show business. Women did not work as cowhands in the wild and woolly West. They certainly didn't have their own brands or trail their cattle to the railhead. In fact— or so one recent history of ranch life proclaims—the cowgirl as "a species" was "unknown on the range" in the mid- to late nineteenth century. "Cowgirls did not ride up the Chisholm Trail," other experts say, for "there just weren't that many women west of the Mississippi" in those heroic early days. And the few who did come west were scarcely suited to the rough life of the plains. "The typical ranch woman [of the Canadian northwest] did little outside work except for occasional flower-gardening," one historian solemnly explains. The real work of the West, it seems, was done by real men. The boldest of women stayed safely indoors, close to their tea sets.

Someone should have explained all this to Lizzie Johnson Williams. Born in Missouri sometime in the 1840s, the young Elizabeth Johnson arrived in Hays County, Texas, in 1852. (By this time, women already accounted for 46.5 per cent of the state's white residents, according to the census.) Educated at private schools, Lizzie quickly established herself as a schoolmarm and, incongruously, as the author of sensational romance stories for *Frank Leslie's Illustrated Weekly* magazine. Bankrolled by her literary successes, Miss Johnson soon bought her way into the cattle business. By 1871, just a few years after the first longhorns headed up the Chisholm Trail, she had acquired land, cattle and the registered CY brand. "She was smart," one oldtimer recalled. "Knew cattle; knew when to buy and when to sell. She always bought good stock."

FACING PAGE. Men have crowded the frame of Western historical writing, and women have had a hard time getting into the picture. *C. D. Kirkland photo, Wyoming Division of Cultural Resources*

Clever, strong-willed Lizzie Williams (1843–1924) was one of Texas's most successful cattle dealers and entre-preneurs. *Austin History Center, Austin Public Library PICB 01490*

Julio Michaud y Thomas created this image for his *Album Pintoresco de la Republica Mexicana* in 1848. His caption—"engraving of a wealthy landowner and his overseer with a general view of Jalapa, Mexico"—noticeably fails to draw attention to the woman in the center of his composition. *Institute of Texan Cultures, San Antonio, Texas*

This was more than could be said, apparently, for the Reverend Hezekiah Williams, the charming, drink-loving clergyman whom Lizzie took as her husband in 1879. As a condition of their union, Hezekiah signed an agreement that gave his wife sole control of her own property, including any she might acquire during their marriage. Although the couple ranched together near Austin and shared the same foreman, they managed their cattle as separate operations. Ever on the lookout for a way to get ahead, they are both said to have instructed their staff to steal good-looking calves from the other's herd. But poor old Hezekiah still couldn't prosper. A risk-taker, with little of Lizzie's good hard sense, he was often forced to turn to her for help with his cattle debts. She never failed to bail him out—and never failed to insist on repayment.

Sometime in the 1880s, Lizzie Williams decided to pursue her business interests to their logical extent by following her herd up the Chisholm Trail to the cattle market in Kansas. Swaddled in skirts, petticoats, bonnet and shawl, she clambered into the seat of her buggy and, with Hezekiah at her side, embarked on months of arduous travel, in sun, rain, wind and dust. According to family tradition, she had the time of her life and, years afterwards, loved to tell how she had tied her blankets around her at night to keep rattlesnakes out of her bed. Every morning before the cattle were stirring, she was out with her tally book, making sure that all of her cows could be accounted for. In another notebook, she carefully recorded each cowhand's hours. "When the herd reached the end of the trail," her biographers tell us, "Lizzie was there, counting up her tallies and estimating her profits."

Lizzie Williams was one of a kind, but she was also one of a breed. Women had owned their own ranches and herds since the earliest days of the North American cattle industry. A list of ranchers in Spanish Texas—those "legitimately engaged in the business of raising cattle" in 1795—includes the names of ten widows. Together, these ladies held title to more than one in five of the early cattle spreads. Although many of them probably relied on males to manage their interests, others reached for the nearest *reata*, swung into the saddle and took care of business themselves. The Doña María del Carmen Calvillo inherited her *rancho* from her father in 1814 and is said to have cut a fine figure as she flew across her lands on her white stallion, issuing instructions to her crew of cowhands. A superb rider and markswoman, she was noted (and tut-tutted) for her flowing black hair, her scandalous male attire and her financial success.

As Anglo settlers moved into Texas in the middle years of the nineteenth century, women continued to found and own ranches, both on their own and in partnership with men. The Little Burke Ranch of 1835, for example, was originally intended as a husband-and-wife operation, but its founder, Ann Burke of Tipperary, Ireland, was widowed during the voyage to America. Despite the birth of a child "only one hour after the ship reached American shores on the Texas coast," she went on to raise cattle and horses on a large land grant in Bee County.

Adeline Hinton of Gonzales County was somewhat luckier. She and her husband established their ranch together in the 1870s. But when cattle had to be trailed to distant rail lines, her husband was often forced to leave for months at a time. Like many another Texas cattlewoman, Adeline managed the ranch—and a family of ten—during his absences. "I know I have baked a thousand biscuits for his trips," another ranch wife recalled. "The time he spent on the trail seemed very long to me, as I stayed at home, took care of the babies and the place."

Since a woman's place was safe at home (where there was nothing to worry about except sick children, cattle rustlers and ornery steers), ladies were generally not encouraged to join in the dangerous adventure of the cattle drive. But like Lizzie Williams, some of them did not wait around for encouragement. They got packed and hit the trail. For the most part, these women just went along for the ride and a few of them—like Amanda Burks, who accidentally set a prairie fire—became a huge nuisance. But others, including Anna Slaughter, who was assigned the job of finding water and campsites for the outfit, managed to make themselves entirely useful.

A handful of women even made the trip as cowhands. Molly Goodnight, co-founder with her husband Charles of the famous JA Ranch in the Texas Panhandle, rode the trail to Dodge City at least twice. A progressive rancher and one of the first to take an interest in purebred cattle, Molly owned her own herds as well as those she shared with her husband. And the honeymooning Belle Barton, who "could ride the wildest 'buckskin' . . . and knew all the tricks of the round-ups," helped drive 500 cattle (her wedding gift from her dad) from central Texas to

Two women posed proudly beside their herd of well-fed horses. *National Archives of Canada PA20580*

5

VIVE LA DIFFÉRENCE!

The golden age of the cowboy spanned less than twenty-five years. It began in 1866, when the first crews of mounted cowhands were hired to drive longhorn cattle up the trail, from the plains of southwest Texas to the western terminus of the rail line (then in Kansas). From there, the animals were shipped to the cities of the northeast, where they satisfied a growing demand for fresh beef. By the late 1880s, when the trail drives came to an end, a total of nine million Texas longhorns had made the long trek north. While most had been sent to market, others had been released onto the "virgin" prairie of the American and Canadian West, as part of the northward expansion of the cattle business. Here, as on the trail, the cattle were supervised by crews of lonely, dirty, poorly paid hands, who have since become the romantic cowboys of popular legend.

Women *were* involved in these early phases of the cattle industry, but not (so far as we know) in large numbers. Their participation really belongs to a slightly later era, which began in the 1870s, hit its stride in the 1890s and continues to the present. During this period, affordable parcels of western land became available for ownership by families and individuals. Although the women who lived on these holdings did not often work for pay, thousands of them worked with cattle as part of their contribution to the family livelihood. These are the women who have inspired the cowgirl legend.

The cowgirl's story is different from the cowboy's, but it is no less important or enjoyable. *Ernest Brown photo, B178, Provincial Archives of Alberta*

Every cattle owner has his or her own brand, a personal "trademark" that is seared into the hide of the cattle. Women in Texas have held registered brands since the late 1700s, including these early examples.

"*For what woman, youthful and full of spirit and the love of living, needs sympathy because of availing herself of the opportunity of being with her husband while at his chosen work in the great out-of-door world?*"
—AMANDA BURKS, ABOUT HER TRIP UP THE
CHISHOLM TRAIL, 1871

COWBOY JO

IN 1904, THE *BOISE CITY CAPITAL NEWS* reported the death of Jo Monaghan, "a well-known character" who had worked, ranched and ridden roundups in Idaho for more than thirty years. Deemed likeable, if a little odd, by his neighbors, Jo had never given anyone reason to suspect that he was actually a woman. He had even enjoyed such exclusively male privileges as voting and serving on juries. But then he died, and the truth was disclosed.

Back in Jo's shack, neighbors found a bundle of letters written over the years by a sister in Buffalo. From them, it emerged that the young Josephine had been cast out by her parents because of an unwelcome pregnancy. Leaving her baby son in the care of her sister, she (now he) headed west in 1867, ending up at Ruby City, Idaho, where she tried her skill at mining and sheep herding. When her disinterest in the bars and dance halls made her conspicuous, she decided to prove up on land of her own and establish a small ranch. Despite the betrayal of a friend who stole almost two decades of savings, she eventually succeeded and, at the time of her death, owned several hundred head of cattle and horses that carried her JO brand. In 1993, her story was told in a revisionist western, *The Ballad of Little Jo.*

Kansas. Her baby daughter rode comfortably in the chuckwagon, in the tender care of the cook.

But the finest adventure of all was reserved for a youngster named Willie Matthews. In 1884, a trail boss called Sam Houston rode into Clayton, New Mexico, looking to hire a couple of hands. Nobody was available except a kid, so Houston signed him on and put him in charge of the horses. For the next three or four months, everything went just right. As Houston remembered it, "the kid would get up the darkest stormy nights and stay with the cattle until the storm was over. He was good natured, very modest, didn't use any cuss words or tobacco, and [was] always pleasant . . . I was so pleased with him that I wished many times that I could find two or three more like him."

Then one evening, about sundown, the boss and the rest of the boys were all sitting around camp when, to Houston's utter bewilderment, he looked up and "saw a lady, all dressed up, coming toward camp . . . Our eyes were all set on her, and every man holding his breath. When she got up within about twenty feet of me, she began to laugh, and said, 'Mr. Houston, you don't know me, do you?'

"Well, for one minute I couldn't speak. She reached her hand out to me, to shake hands, and I said, 'Kid, is it possible that you are a lady?'" And, of course, it was. Willie (Wilhelmina?) Matthews had grown up on her father's intoxicating stories of the old cow trails of the 1870s and had made up her mind to relive his adventures. Outfitting herself in her brother's clothes, she had ridden over from Kansas to meet the herds and get a job as a cowpuncher. "I am glad I found you," she told Houston in parting, "for I have enjoyed myself."

We will never know how many cowboys were, in fact, cowgirls enjoying themselves, but Willie Matthews could not have been the only one. The story went around, for example, of a young woman—jilted on the way to the altar—who followed her false lover onto the cattle range. Disguised as a man, she worked as a cowboy for months, "riding horseback as reckless and fast" as the best of them. When she finally met up with her ex-boyfriend, she took him off by himself, then "drew her revolver and made herself known to him." Although she refused to say exactly what happened next, she was mightily pleased with the result. "I'll bet he won't trifle with another girl's affection," she told the press. "I am satisfied, and am going home."

Other women had less melodramatic reasons for working the west in drag. Teenage girls in the California gold mines wore boys' clothes in order to avoid sexual attention and, perhaps, to increase their chances of getting employed. Mrs. E. J. Guerin, who lived as "Mountain Charley" for thirteen years in the 1840s and 1850s, saw cross-dressing "as the only resort from starvation or worse." A destitute young widow with children to support, she decided to pass as a man in order to seek a livelihood "among the avenues which are so religiously closed against my sex." Dressed in pants, she owned and operated saloons, worked on the railways and drove cattle across the continent. In time, "I began to rather like the freedom of my new character," she admitted. "I could go where I chose, [and] do many things which while innocent in themselves, were debarred by propriety from association with the female sex"—such as earning a decent wage.

It seems entirely possible that other women worked the cattle drives as cowboys and then quietly went home, taking care that their secret did not become known. A few women did something even more outrageous. They got themselves hired in the Texas cattle trade as women. The *Denver Times*, for example, published the story of Miss Fanny Seabride, who came to Texas from Chicago in the 1890s to take up the demure calling of governess. But, as luck would have it, she was out at "the famous Horseshoe XX ranch" one day when a fence rider was thrown off his horse and hurt. Who would go and fix a break in the fence some thirty miles away? Why, Miss Seabride, of course. Before anyone could stop her, she had leaped aboard a mustang and, "with hatchet, wire, staples and a rifle lashed to her saddle, she galloped away and repaired the damage." Having thus demonstrated her skills, the governess-gone-wild immediately applied for the post left vacant by the bucked-off cowboy. "After trying to frighten the girl by telling her of the wild animals she would be expected to fight, the [ranch owner] gave her permission to ride until she was tired." Four years later, when the *Times* caught up with her, she could claim to have performed her duties well and also to have proven herself as a bounty hunter, having "killed and scalped 531 coyotes, forty-nine lobo wolves, thirty-nine wildcats, thirteen jougars [whatever they were] and two black bears." With her savings, she had purchased a thousand head of cattle and was confidently preparing to establish "a thoroughly equipped ranch of her own earning."

The land Miss Seabride had leased for her ranch was not in Texas but out on the western plains. Although the southern ranch industry continued to develop throughout the century and

A downcast Monica Hopkins posed with skins and trophies from animals that were shot on the family ranch near Priddis, Alberta, about 1910. *Glenbow Archives, Calgary, Alberta, PA397-19*

FACING PAGE. "I'll bet he won't trifle with another girl's affection," the cowgirl told the press. (This image was reproduced by several postcard publishers in the early 1900s.)

Of all the interesting and accomplished women who lived in cattle country, only two would ever be fully admitted to Wild West mythology. Although neither was a cowgirl in the strict sense of the word, their reputations as "gender outlaws" would eventually help to shape the cowgirl legend. They were Belle Starr and Calamity Jane.

BELLE STARR (born Myra Bell Shirley in 1848) had the misfortune to live in dangerous times. A passionate supporter of the Confederate side in the American Civil War, she was a friend of the "outlaw" gangs of southern partisans. Later, through her second husband, Sam Starr, she was drawn into the political tensions of life in the Indian Territory. Although she was once convicted of horse theft, her life of crime really began after her death, in the pages of a false and sensational pamphlet about her life. Today, the legendary Bandit Queen continues to live in the images of a dozen films and TV programs.

CALAMITY JANE, on the other hand, fictionalized her own life. Her self-penned "Life and Adventures" are bursting with boastful talk about her fabulous exploits and her famous associates. But the bare facts of her story are also impressive. Born Martha Jane Cannary in 1852, she arrived in Montana as a young teenager. When her parents died soon thereafter, she was left to fend for herself. An expert horsewoman, she found work as a teamster and, at times, as an army scout. A hard worker and a hard drinker, she died in middle age, leaving behind a reputation that has inspired dozens of dime-novel stories and more than twenty screen portraits.

Richard K. Fox of New York published a scurrilous biography of Belle Starr in 1889, which established her reputation as an outlaw. *Denver Public Library, Western History Collection*

RIGHT AND FACING PAGE. Calamity Jane launched her own legend by selling photos of herself as a frontierswoman. By the 1950s, when *Comet* featured her, she was often portrayed as a western Peter Pan. *Buffalo Bill Historical Center, Cody, Wyoming*

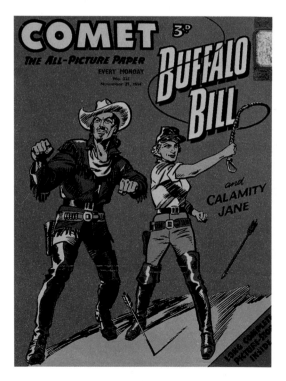

the long cattle drives persisted until 1890, big money and big ambition increasingly turned their attention farther north. From the 1870s on, the real excitement lay on the newly opened ranges of Wyoming, Montana, Colorado, Alberta and Saskatchewan. An endless sea of windswept pasturelands was virtually free for the taking, and the press burbled about the fortunes that were to be made in the "beef bonanza." In the heady enthusiasm of the moment, the prior claims of First Nations peoples and the inconvenient presence of several million buffalo could be brushed aside as minor hindrances to the unstoppable course of moneymaking.

The first to strike it rich on the western range were well-heeled capitalists and consortia—the cattle barons of western legend—who acquired vast areas of public lands on which to run huge free-ranging herds. With very few exceptions, these large, corporate-style holdings were owned and managed by males and staffed with male cowhands. Not surprisingly, the census-takers counted four men for every woman in Montana and Wyoming in

In the late nineteenth century, the Aboriginal hunting culture of the plains was displaced by the herding culture of the ranchers. Kitsipimi Otunna, a Sarcee woman from southern Alberta, and this "ranche" near Calgary were both photographed around 1890. *Ernest Brown photos, BF1 and B124, Provincial Archives of Alberta*

1870. But by the 1880s (a little later in Canada), these male-dominated enterprises were increasingly challenged by an influx of smallholders and homesteaders, who struggled to assert a rival claim to water and rangeland. By and large, these ranches were, or soon became, family operations that included women.

In the 1880s and 1890s, women flooded west by the thousands, and the skewed sex ratios of the early days began to swing quite rapidly towards equality. Something like 100,000 women (and 160,000 men) surged into the cow country of Montana and Wyoming in just two decades. In the yellowing pages of western histories, these women have been recalled with tender sentiment as Gentle Tamers, Pioneers in Petticoats, Saints in Sunbonnets and Madonnas of the Prairie. What a trial it must have been for them, we are invited to reflect—all those proper nineteenth-century ladies who bravely faced the insult of a rude and untamed land. Instinctive homebodies, they were nonetheless cruelly torn from their families, friends and familiar comforts. Yet what could a lady do except to follow her lord and master wherever he might lead, even if it be into darkest Wyoming? A womanly woman had no choice but to go and meekly suffer the consequences of loneliness, overwork and deprivation, even as she labored to bring beauty and grace to her new home. Her martyrdom became her heroism.

Like most stereotypes, this image of the Noble Pioneer Woman is both seductive and laughable. Certainly, settlers of both sexes survived hardships as they established themselves in the West. Life and work were often brutal, perhaps especially so for women. In addition to the continuous physical labor, in which everyone shared, women faced the additional difficulties

ALTHOUGH LARGE CORPORATE-STYLE ranches rarely hired women to work with stock, there were exceptions. According to a report in *The North British Agriculturalist*, Middy Morgan was an Irish gentlewoman fallen on hard times, who came to America in search of work as a governess. When that plan failed ("the New York ladies, who have to suffer from the tyranny of Irish cooks and housemaids, object entirely to Irish governesses"), she headed west and took work as a hired girl. "In a short time she had acquired so much skill in the breeding and rearing of stock that the farmer, perceiving her value, admitted her to a partnership in the farm." With that backing, she went on to become known and respected as a judge of cattle. "At every great fair or market may she be seen . . . with a long cowhide whip in hand, wending her way with skill between the droves." Impressed by her reputation and judgement, the Earl of Dunmore hired Miss Morgan to select the stock for his new cattle ranch in Montana in 1880.

13

of childbirth and childcare. (Recalling her pioneer childhood in the 1840s, Martha Ann Morrison came to the conclusion that "Mothers . . . had to undergo more trial and suffering than anybody else.") Many women were also pained by the crudeness of their lives, so unlike the lily-white, ladylike ideal to which they aspired. ("I have cooked so much out in the sun and smoke, that I hardly know who I am," mourned Miriam Davis in 1855. "[W]hen I look into the little looking glass I ask, 'Can this be me?'")

But if emigrant women were often anxious about losing their "womanliness," some of them were also anxious *to* lose it or, at least (like Mountain Charley before them), to escape from the most aggravating limitations of Victorian femininity. Almost from the beginning, the West offered unusual opportunities to aspiring females. Wyoming Territory, for example, was the first jurisdiction in North America to enact women's suffrage (1869), appoint a female justice of the peace (Esther Morris, in 1870), welcome a woman into the state legislature (Mary Bellamy, in 1910) and induct a female governor (Nellie Taylor Ross, in 1925). Other western states and provinces, though they lagged behind Wyoming's trail-blazing example, were generally well ahead of their eastern counterparts. In 1913, several years before suffrage was finally extended to women throughout the United States, Theodore Roosevelt quipped, "I think civilization is coming Eastward gradually."

Western jurisdictions were also among the first to establish the legal right of married women to their own incomes and lands. In an appeal to bachelor-members of the California legislature in 1849, one lawmaker argued that improved property laws "offer a great inducement for women of fortune" to come west and become wives. But western wives, once gotten, did not always stay married, for the divorce laws of most western states were also relatively generous. Not only were the grounds for the divorce quite broad—impotence, adultery, desertion, drunkenness and cruelty, among others—but the courts were liberal in their interpretation of women's grievances. Around Helena, Montana, between 1865 and 1870, for example, one divorce was granted for every three marriages, and almost all the dissolutions were instigated by women. In 1853, Abby Mansur confided to her sister that she might just look around for a richer spouse, on the grounds that "it is all the go here for Lady's to leave there Husbands."

But the real lure of the West, for women as for men, was the promise of free land. As early as 1862, homesteads, preemptions and other land grants in the western states were available to any female who was the head of her own household, be she single, widowed, divorced—even a runaway wife—provided that she could meet certain residency requirements. As one commen-

Excited by the wide-open possibilities of the West, Kitty Tatch and her friend danced a jig on Overhanging Rock at Glacier Point in Yosemite National Park. *Yosemite NPS Research Library*

FACING PAGE. The stereotype of the wistful, patient pioneer woman was perfectly captured by William Henry David Koerner in his 1921 painting *Madonna of the Prairie. Buffalo Bill Historical Center, Cody, Wyoming*

"The chief figure of the American West, the figure of the ages is . . . the gaunt and sad-faced woman sitting on the front seat of the wagon, following her lord where he might lead."
—EMERSON HOUGH, 1921

CHEYENNE

(SHY ANN)

SONG

WORDS BY
HARRY WILLIAMS

JEROME H. REMICK & CO.

5

tator put it, men and women "were appallingly equal" under the U.S. Homestead Act—"equal labor, equal privation and equal failure—or victory." A surprisingly large number of women were willing to take the chance, in both farm and ranch country. In parts of Wyoming, for example, the proportion of single women who settled on homesteads averaged about 12 percent through the 1890s, and most of them succeeded in gaining title to their land. Writing from South Dakota in 1905, one settler commented, "There are the most old maids out here holding down claims that a person must wonder where they all come from."

Single women homesteaders seem to have been ambitious for land and a measure of independence. E. J. Wilder, for example, settled in the Dakota Territory in 1879 to fulfill a childhood desire to own her own home. Five years later, Mary O'Kieffe ditched a good-for-nothing husband and moved westward in order to "start all over in a new country under what she hoped would be more favorable conditions and where at least she would have greater freedom." Wyoming homesteader Elinore Pruitt Stewart agreed to marry her neighbor but on condition that, as she put it, "I should meet all my land difficulties unaided. I wanted the fun and the experience." Vesta Keen came looking for a chance to ride astride and to vote; Mary Price Jeffords simply could "not see why a girl could not do anything a boy could do."

For every woman who homesteaded on her own, there were, of course, many others who settled with their husbands and children. Whether they wished to or not, these women often found themselves stepping over the traces of feminine decorum and adopting a position of greater (if far from perfect) equality with their menfolk. Under "civilized" conditions back East, ladies and gentlemen attempted to stay within separate spheres—women confined to the home, men at large in the world. But on a struggling ranch, this rigid division of labor was hopelessly inappropriate. There was work to be done, and woman-power at hand to do it. So wives and daughters scrubbed, canned, baked, gardened, sewed, milked, hauled water, chopped wood, doctored the sick, taught the kids, and did whatever else was necessary to keep the house and household running as smoothly as possible. But few had the option of devoting themselves solely to domestic pursuits.

Sebina Jacobson and Johanna Solberg each had a homestead of her own near a place called Square Deal, Alberta. *Glenbow Archives, Calgary, Alberta, NA206-27*

FACING PAGE. The hit song "Cheyenne/Shy Ann," first published in 1905, tells the story of a woman who is bullied into marrying her cowboy suitor. But the cowgirl on the cover of the sheet music looks capable of bringing about a happier ending. *Courtesy of Mary Schmitt, Teton Village, Wyoming*

LET ER' RARE

The men "made you mad. You just felt like telling them to go to Hell. [But] they wasn't bossing me. I was on my own. They must have thought I was a tough old sassy thing, but I didn't care what they thought. I had to fight my own battles. I didn't ask them for help."

—SOUTH DAKOTA WOMAN HOMESTEADER

"Petticoats are no bar to progress in either writing or ranching," Wyoming's Caroline Lockhart once said. Nor, she might have added, do they keep you from having fun. A stockgrower, civic leader, newspaperwoman and best-selling novelist, Caroline had a hearty taste for the pleasures of western life, including liquor, lovers and rodeo. (The sign on the front of the bar reads "Spit in the Box.") *Buffalo Bill Historical Center, Cody, Wyoming*

FACING PAGE. Two "cowgirls," one from Illinois and one from Idaho, clowned for the camera in 1898. *American Heritage Center, University of Wyoming*

When Catherine Neil arrived from Scotland to join her new husband on a sheep ranch in southern Alberta in 1905, she found herself thinking fondly of her days back home, where she had lain in bed till eight. Here, she found herself living in a range camp, climbing out of a tent at 4:30 AM to make breakfast and then, while her husband was eating, riding out across the hills to bring in the sheep. At lambing time, it was she who carried the lambs into the tent and warmed them beside the oven. "When a ewe could not lamb herself, perhaps by reason of the lamb coming wrong or the legs twisted, my duty was to assist, as I had a smaller hand." At shearing time, she turned the grindstone while her husband sharpened the shears. "I would turn and turn until my arms were so tired I could have cried, but if I said one of the men might do it, I got the answer that sheep shearing for a whole day was no boy's job and the men were tired. So as mother's work is never done, . . . I turned and turned."

Monica Hopkins, who arrived on an Alberta ranch in 1909 with her sunshade and the social graces of a clergyman's daughter, cheerfully threw herself into the hard physical labor of her duties as a ranch wife. But, robust young person that she was, she just couldn't find enough to keep her busy. Casting about for worthwhile occupations, she concluded that the only option was to work with her husband. "I am afraid that I am rather inclined to spend more time than I should outside with Billie, helping him when I can," she confessed in a letter home. Although she adored animals and outdoor life, she nonetheless felt squeamish about her adoption of "male" concerns. "This is essentially a man's country," she wrote, and "a woman has practically to sink her own identity and take on her husband's interests."

However much they may have enjoyed their newfound competence, many of the women who came west as adults were troubled by the loss of their womanly dignity. Not so their daughters. Girls who grew up on the range, for the most part, were unabashedly in love with

"For the woman with outdoor propensities and a taste for roughing it there is no life more congenial than that of the saddle and rifle, as it may still be lived in parts of the Western States."
—EVELYN CAMERON, 1906

"I have tried every kind of work this ranch affords, and I can do any of it. Of course I am extra strong, but those who try know that strength and knowledge come with doing. I just love to experiment, to work, and to prove out things, so that ranch life and 'roughing it' just suit me."
—ELINORE PRUITT STEWART, 1913

Letter from a Lady Rancher

I find that another pair of hands can be very useful around a corral, not to mention a pair of legs to "run and fetch things." It's a case of "Hold this halter while I tie Buck's feet," or "Can you steady the log while I hang this gate?" I have heated branding irons in a fire while Billie has roped and tied a calf that he is turning out on the range with its mother. I have also helped Billie brand Buck, that is, Billie did the branding, I handed the red hot iron to him and felt like the Lord High Executioner in doing it. Billie says it doesn't hurt the animal very much if the iron is good and red, but I don't know, I'd hate to have it done to me. But I must confess that it doesn't seem to bother the animal very much after the first jump; just as soon as they are let out of the "squeeze" their first idea is to nibble at the grass.

So you see I'm quite useful. Generally these jobs, according to Billie, only take "two minutes" but I usually find that 30 minutes are nearer the mark. I suddenly realize that it is getting on to lunch time and nothing is ready so I dash to the house to catch up with my own work.

—Monica Hopkins, Priddis, Alberta, 1911

FAR LEFT. Although Monica Hopkins preferred to think of herself as her husband's assistant, she was entirely capable of doing ranch work on her own. This photograph, taken about 1910, shows her halterbreaking a colt, much to the detriment of her long skirts. *Glenbow Archives, Calgary, Alberta, PA397-16*

CENTER AND RIGHT. Evelyn Cameron was brought up as a proper English gentlewoman, but she cheerfully gave up the pleasures of upper-class life, including her elegant sidesaddle (bottom), for the adventure of homesteading in Montana. The self-portrait on the right, taken in 1904, shows her making bread in her kitchen. A few years later, she attributed her superb health to her life in the open air and the benefits of hard work. *Evelyn Cameron photos, Montana Historical Society*

BELOW. The ladies in this turn-of-the-century hunting party look as comfortable with their firearms as they do with their frypan. *Ernest Brown photo, B6467, Provincial Archives of Alberta*

their unconventional lives. A case in point was Agnes Morley, who arrived on a cattle ranch in New Mexico in the late 1880s, aged 11. Here, to her open-mouthed delight (and her lady-mother's dismay), dinner-table conversation focused on the latest lynching in the neighborhood and the recent shooting death of Billy the Kid. "For us children . . . the new life was from the beginning a sort of glorified picnic."

Although Mother Morley did her best to run the ranch on her own (having been widowed and deserted in quick succession), she was actually more interested in corresponding with her friend Susan B. Anthony and keeping in touch with womanly culture back East. So, while the two worthy ladies shared their thoughts on the emancipation of women, Agnes turned her attention to a more muscular mode of equity. "The cattle business in those days was conducted on horseback," she recalled. "Any rider who knew what to do was on a parity with any other rider who knew what to do . . . Although I rode sidesaddle like a lady, the double standard did not exist . . . Up to the point of my actual physical limitations I worked side by side with the men, receiving the same praise or same censure for like undertakings." Her job, as she saw it, was simply "to 'make a hand,' thereby saving the wages of a man."

This she did, and with pizazz. "In fact, after fifty years, I vaingloriously affirm that I enjoyed a local reputation in the one field where reputations most counted—that of good horsemanship. To prove it, I cherished for years a clipping from *Mine and Lariat*, an early

With their father absent on roundups and other business for half the year, the Buckley sisters ran a Montana ranch with their mother, in the years before the First World War. *Evelyn Cameron photo, Montana Historical Society*

OVERLEAF. Children on pioneer farms and ranches learned to ride and work with animals almost as soon as they could walk. The child on the right, sitting on the pig, was named Katie Daniothy. *Glenbow Archives, Calgary, Alberta, NC39-295 and NC39-302*

"I guess I drove more cattle, broke more horses and ran more races than any woman I ever knew. But do you know, when I rounded up and drove cattle for Frye and Company they wouldn't list a woman's name on the payroll? I got my wages, though."
—VIVIAN THORP McCLAREY

This unidentified woman worked on the Pitchfork Ranch in Wyoming. *C. J. Belden photo, American Heritage Center, University of Wyoming*

weekly paper . . . It informed our local reading public that 'Miss Agnes of the Datils and Three-Fingered Pete are the best riders in the country.'"

Rancher Ann Bassett Willis was born into the "bronco West" of western Colorado in 1878. By her own telling, she "began life as a cow hand at the mature age of six" and counted herself as part of "a new generation, radically different from their New England ancestors," who "kept the parents in a state of mental agitation. We were completely western by birth and environment, actively disliking anything that resembled a pattern."

As a child, she remembered, "I turned a deaf ear to mother's long-winded lectures upon the conduct of, and correct clothing for, 'little ladies,' and early adopted buckskin breeches for my personal use . . . I cared not a whit for social customs, and could not understand a world designed especially for privileged little boys to romp in, to enjoy sports and play, sternly denied to 'little ladies.' With spirit and determination I wore my befringed, buckskin breeches. My point was difficult to prove in a puritanical sphere where girls' legs were strictly hush-hush, and anything resembling trousers for women or girls was taboo . . . However—the buckskins won out."

"[T]he grown-ups' agony over such 'disgraceful' apparel was pathetic," Ann recalled. Indeed, in society at large there was much hand-wringing and distress about women's smouldering interest in "bifurcated" garments. The notorious "bloomer" costume—a pair of pantaloons worn under a short dress—had been introduced by eastern feminists in 1851, as a healthful and progressive alternative to the long, heavy skirts and whalebone corsets then in style. Despite a brief flurry of interest (notably among women who were making the trek west), the "reform dress" aroused such ferocious hostility that even its sponsor, the courageous Amelia Bloomer, quickly abandoned it.

MOTHER.

In 1911, Mrs. Lindsay D. Elliott of the Kneehill Ranch near Carbon, Alberta still preferred her sidesaddle and long riding skirts, choices that identified her as a dignified (and perhaps wealthy) woman. But the cowgirl in her work clothes, below, had also achieved a measure of respectability and recognition. *Left, Glenbow Archives, Calgary, Alberta, NA4657-5* OVERLEAF. On the wild and windswept plains, six women shooters steadied their aim. *Buffalo Bill Historical Center, Cody, Wyoming, private collection*

Cowgirl, Western Canada

According to the *New York Times* of May 27, 1876, any woman who "thirst[ed] for trousers" was mentally ill, the victim of a "curious mental disorder" that involved hysteria and hallucinations. But the girls and women who worked with cattle on the great western plains weren't hallucinating about their need for practical work clothing. Some of them found a semi-ladylike compromise in the "California riding costume," a voluminous divided skirt crafted of leather. Hot and heavy, with a tendency to scare green horses by flapping about, divided skirts were a poor substitute for pants, but at least they looked like dresses when the wearer was on the ground. Yet even this decorous costume could arouse "a small sensation," as Montana rancher Evelyn Cameron discovered when she wore hers into town. "So great at first was the prejudice against any divided garment in Montana that a warning was given me to abstain from riding on the streets of Miles City lest I might be arrested! After riding into town forty-eight miles from the ranch, I was much amused at the laughing and giggling girls who stood staring at my costume as I walked about." Another woman remembered wearing a split skirt when she drove cattle, but being sent home when the herd reached town so that her shameful garb couldn't be noticed.

By wearing divided garments, ranch girls and women prepared themselves for yet another outrage. They mounted their horses man-style, with the horse securely between their legs. By contrast, a proper lady—a "real girl," in Ann Willis's mocking phrase—kept her limbs tightly together and clung to a sidesaddle, a miserable "one-sided thing" that subjected the horses to "back-eating kidney sores and galled withers." Evelyn Cameron, who had been accustomed to ride sidesaddle in England and still deemed it her "first love," nonetheless believed that the man's saddle was superior "for all [the] kinds of work on horseback performed by women in Western America." The faint of heart, as always,

Wearing split skirts or pants was an act of "everyday rebellion" that women had to commit over and over again, each in her own household or community. By the 1920s, west Texas rancher Hallie Crawford Stillwell (center) and her friends were free to enjoy the practicality and comfort of lightweight divided skirts. *Courtesy of Linda Perron*

Was It Decadence?

My own great concession to a new age was to abandon the sidesaddle. Why, for ten years, I continued to ride sidesaddle is a mystery to me now. I recall the steps that led to emancipation.

First, I discarded, or rather refused to adopt, the sunbonnet, conventional headgear of my female neighbors. When I went unashamedly about under a five-gallon (not ten-gallon) Stetson, many an eyebrow was raised; then followed a double-breasted blue flannel shirt, with white pearl buttons, frankly unfeminine. In time came blue denim knickers worn *under* a short blue denim skirt. Slow evolution (or was it decadence?) toward a costume suited for immediate needs. Decadence having set in, the descent from the existing standards of female modesty to purely human comfort and convenience was swift. A man's saddle and a divided skirt (awful monstrosity that it was) were inevitable. This was in the middle nineties.

"I won't ride in the same cañon with you," protested [brother] Ray, when I first appeared thus clad.

"Put that promise in writing—you might forget it," I snapped.

And forget it he did. Vehemently he denied only a few months later ever having said it, wherein he was not unlike many another penitent who has rushed into delivering a premature ultimatum.

—Agnes Morley Cleaveland

In 1922, the women's leather riding skirt pictured at the top of the page was available through Riley and McCormick Ltd. of Calgary for the handsome sum of $25. At about the same time, a pair of ladies' spurs cost a mere $9. *Glenbow Archives, Calgary, Alberta*

LEFT. When seen through a stereoscopic viewer, this hand-colored card offered a 3-D view of a "typical" western girl. *Buffalo Bill Historical Center, Cody, Wyoming*

Back in the Saddle Again

FACING PAGE. Joyce Burton hogties a calf on the V-Bar-T Ranch, near Medicine Hat, Alberta, 1943.

Richard Wright, National Archives of Canada PA116129

were shocked, but what was a person to do? A new country called for new actions. Once women were sensibly garbed and mounted for life on the range, "the cowgirl was a necessary consequence, and the side-saddle [had] passed into ancient history" by the turn of the century.

Thus, the cowgirl—the tough, outdoorsy girl or woman who loved riding horses and working with livestock—was born on the family ranches of western America. Unlike the cowboy, who signed up as a wage laborer, the cowgirl earned her spurs, for the most part, as an unpaid worker who contributed her efforts as a wife or, more often, as a daughter. Of course, this didn't happen on every spread. Some females continued to define themselves primarily as housekeepers, either through choice or through family preference. But others saddled up their broncos and rode out with the herds. Thoroughly versed in domestic chores, they could whip up a three-egg cake or turn a tidy hem, but they were happiest on horseback, holding the herd at the branding or riding the roundup. In some neighborhoods, such "cowboy girls" were scarce, but in many localities it was common for girls to work with cattle. "An awful lot of the girls I knew rode," reported Marie Bell of Iron Mountain, Wyoming. Some of them even went from ranch to ranch, breaking horses for pay. "I don't know what they charged. Sometimes they would take a horse in trade for breaking several. They were very nice girls. It was just a case of making some money, and that's the only way they had."

For the girls themselves, it was all quite matter-of-fact. Whether the task at hand was gathering wild horses or dragging a mired cow out of the mud, "we just did it," another ranch girl said. "That's what we had to do, so we did it." Although well aware of their sins against convention (their critics saw to that), they were remarkably unrepentant and unabashed. When the occasion warranted, they could dress up and "be" a lady with the best of them. In their own estimation, at least, the fact that they happened to be crack shots or to bust broncs did not "unsex" them. As Ann Willis put it, "I suggest that it is not the range on which she moves, but her brand, that identifies the heifer. A mere 'hair' brand will shed. It's only the deep-in stay-on kind that really measures up." If the cowboy was nature's gentleman, the cowgirl took her place, in her own mind's eye, as nature's lady.

But however pleased she might be with herself, any woman who broke the rules was open to attack from others. In the gossips' court, a bad girl was a bad girl. Ann Willis felt the sting of *this* brand as a result of her struggle to save her ranch from the big Middlesex Cattle Company. Her enemies hinted that she was "loose" and an "intimate pal" of Butch Cassidy (whom she actually never met). They charged her with cattle theft and whispered that she ran her own gang of bandits (although no case against her could ever be upheld). If a woman wore pants

Ellen Watson, a.k.a. Cattle Kate, was the only woman ever lynched in the western states. She was killed alongside her friend (perhaps husband) Jim Averell.

and spoke up for herself, it was hard to imagine the lengths to which her deviance might extend.

A woman named Ellen Watson of Sweetwater Valley, Wyoming, received even rougher treatment. The only woman to be lynched in the American West, she was killed in 1889 by cattle barons who objected to the location of her homestead. News of her death was first reported by a pro-stockgrower newspaper, the *Cheyenne Daily Leader*, which slandered her as a cattle rustler, whore and "virago" known as Cattle Kate. "Of robust physique she was a daredevil in the saddle, handy with a six-shooter and adept with the lariat and branding iron," the paper cried. Worse yet, "she rode straddle, always had a vicious broncho for a mount and seemed never to tire of dashing across the range." For these "crimes" alone, it seemed to some that her death was justified.

Happily, ranch women usually received a gentler response from both the public and the press. Yes, jaws sometimes dropped when they rode into town; yes, eyebrows were raised. But to many observers there was something admirable about this virile new version of femininity. The ranch woman's vigor, which "under ordinary circumstances" would be "improper and unbecoming," could be seen as "praiseworthy" in this new country, where skill and courage were valued and necessary. When a reporter asked a woman rancher how she kept her cowboys in line, she said, "I suppose it's because they admire pluck." And so, indeed, did the citizens of the young continent. The ranch women of the West pioneered a new style of all-American womanhood, a pragmatic blending of masculine power and "natural" feminine charm. It was a combination that would shortly take the world by storm.

Our Little Cowgirl

(TRADITIONAL WESTERN BALLAD)

Thar she goes a-lopin', stranger,
Khaki-gowned, with flyin' hair,
Talk about your classy ridin',—
Wal, you're gettin' it right thar.
Jest a kid, but lemme tell you
When she warms a saddle seat
On that outlaw bronc a-straddle
She is one that can't be beat!

Ride? Why, she can cut a critter
From the herd as neat as pie,
Read a brand out on the ranges
Just as well as you or I.
Ain't much yet with the riata,
But you give her a few years
And no puncher with the outfit
Will beat her a-ropin' steers.

Proud o' her? Say, lemme tell you,
She's the queen of all the range;
Got a grip upon our heart-strings
Mighty strong, but that ain't strange;
'Cause she loves the lowin' cattle,
Loves the hills and open air,
Dusty trails on blossomed canons
God has strung around out here.

Hoof-beats poundin' down the mesa,
Chicken-time in lively tune,
Jest below the trail to Keeber's,—
Wait, you'll see her pretty soon.
You kin bet I know that ridin',—
Now she's toppin' yonder swell.
Thar she is; that's her a-smilin'
At the bars of the corral.

With her pretty feminine graces and impressive
masculine skills, the cowgirl came to represent a new
and promising ideal of womanhood. *Courtesy of
Barbara Hodgson*
OVERLEAF. Wild West show cowgirl Jane Bernoudy
signed this souvenir photo for a fan in London,
England, probably in the 1890s. *American Heritage
Center, University of Wyoming*

LIVING LEGENDS

Fancy sometimes helps us out

in this big round world.

Phoebe Ann Moses Butler, a.k.a. Annie Oakley

The women and girls who did a "man's job" on the rangelands of the West generally didn't go out of their way to draw attention to themselves. But there were times, in the wide-open spaces of cow country, when it was impossible for a girl to avoid attracting a little friendly notice. Long-time Wyoming rancher Marie Bell remembered a time in the early days when her family's herd was grazing beside a train track and some of the neighbors' cattle got mixed up with them. She and her friend Villa were roping out the strays when they saw a train coming down the line. The next time they glanced up, the train had pulled to a stop, and the passengers were plastered against the windows to have a good gawk. Wait till they told their neighbors back home about seeing cowgirls!

East meets West in this cartoon by Fay King, a commentator for the *New York Daily Mirror*, first published in the program of the Madison Square Garden Rodeo in 1937. *Courtesy of Mary Schmitt, Teton Village, Wyoming*

FACING PAGE. Thousands of western dime novels were published around the turn of the century, and a few of them featured "western Amazons" like Wild Nell, seen here rescuing Buffalo Bill from two of his enemies. *Buffalo Bill Historical Center, Cody, Wyoming*

Cattle Queens with their horses and guns were a marvel of the West, right up there with shaggy bison and "noble savages." By the late nineteenth century, these wonders could be enjoyed by people back East for the price of a train trip or, for those on tighter budgets, the cost of a theater seat. If you couldn't afford to go out west, you had only to wait until its choicest curiosities were reproduced on your very doorstep.

The first person to make a fortune by "performing" the West was a sometime frontiersman and full-time self-promoter named William Frederick Cody, better known as Buffalo Bill. Cody had enjoyed his first tantalizing taste of stardom in 1869, when his name was attached to the hero of a flashy adventure story, *Buffalo Bill, the King of the Border Men*. This led, in short order, to a series of stage appearances in which Cody, impersonating himself, reenacted his exploits from the Indian Wars—suitably enhanced for the theater. (His first night out, he "shot" forty or fifty fake Indians in an uproar of gunshot and smoke.)

To the copywriters who hyped his shows, these productions offered "the most wonderful combination on Earth," with "Real Living Heroes" like Cody and his friend Wild Bill Hickok in "new" and "sensational" dramas about Buffalo Bill's heroic adventures. Here were the genuine and authentic marvels of the still-half-fabulous West, packaged with all the hoopla and flair of a popular entertainment.

Like the barker for a medicine show, Cody toured the United States, peddling this intoxicating mixture of fact and fantasy. Every now and then, he took time out to return west and chalk up a few more splendid accomplishments, which he immediately incorporated into his stage program. In July of 1876, for example, while working as a scout for the Fifth Cavalry, he dressed up in his black-velvet stage costume, killed a Cheyenne chief named Yellow Hand, and claimed his scalp as an act of vengeance for General Custer's death. By October, Yellow Hand's scalp was on display during Buffalo Bill's theatrical "exhibition," available for viewing by anyone who was willing to pay 35 cents.

Cody had found his unique niche in show business. As his ambitions outgrew the confines of the theater, he began to mount spectacular outdoor pageants, complete with buffaloes, bucking broncos, wild longhorns and a cowboy band in shiny white Stetsons. Halfway through the evening performances, real Indians swarmed across the arena to attack an actual Deadwood stagecoach; in the final act, braves in feather headdresses whooped and hollered around a settler's cabin—and who should come thundering to the rescue in both these crises but that veritable American hero, Buffalo Bill Himself, with his cadre of frontiersmen. This was not merely a western circus, Cody insisted; it was the one and only true Wild West, a stirring celebration of the nation's epic accomplishments and masterful character, now packaged for presentation to the world as "America's National Entertainment."

It didn't immediately occur to Cody that women might have a prideful place—or indeed much place at all—in this absolutely authentic commemoration. True, he employed a number of Aboriginal women to represent traditional camp life, but none of them was ever acknowledged by name on posters or programs. Another woman, also anonymous, played the part of the settler's helpless wife, who waited beside her cabin to be rescued by Bill and his gallant cowboys. But the leading figures of Cody's "dramatic-equestrian exhibition" of western history were all men, with white males as heroes, Native Americans as noble savages and Mexican fancy ropers as novelty acts. (The lone African American to appear in the show's first ten seasons was inventively misidentified as an "Indian from Africa.") Like its many imitators on both stage and screen, Buffalo Bill's Wild West was White Man's Territory.

Then, in 1885, just as the show was embarking on its third busy season, one of Cody's top performers, a sharpshooter with the mustachioed handle of Captain Bogardus, suddenly left the company. There to apply for the vacancy was a sometime-circus equestrienne and markswoman who called herself Annie Oakley. Cody was cautious about hiring her—could this tiny creature really withstand the recoil of heavy firearms? And even after he signed her on, he seems to have been uneasy about adding a female headliner to his company. "This little Missie here is Miss Annie Oakley," he told the rest of his outfit. "She's to be the only white woman with our show. And I want you boys to welcome her and protect her."

It is hard to imagine a woman with less need for masculine protection than Annie Oakley. Born in Ohio in 1860, she had been working to support herself since early childhood. From the time I was nine," she once told a friend, "I never had a nickel I did not earn myself." Although skilled as a seamstress and as household help, she was also proficient as a hunter and woodswoman. Indeed, her aim was so true and her kills so clean that her game was soon in great demand by the restaurant trade. By the time she was fifteen, she had a local reputation as a markswoman.

When a team of exhibition sharpshooters came by that year, someone put young Annie forward as a challenger. Not only did she win the match, but she also won the affections of her opponent. Within a year, she and professional crack shot Frank Butler were wed. Although he suggested that she join his shooting act as an on-stage assistant, she insisted that they appear as equals instead. But there was no equality in the audience response to their performances. By the time the Butlers signed on with Buffalo Bill several years later, Frank was the assistant and Annie was the shootist.

In the Wild West arena, Annie Oakley's star shone brighter than ever. Audiences gasped when she drilled a dime out of her husband's hand or flicked the ash off the end of his cigarette. They cheered when she split an apple perched on her dog's head. They fairly raised the roof when she swerved round the ring on her bicycle and shot at moving targets. In one popular stunt, she turned her back on her target, rested her rifle backwards on top of her head, and found her mark by sighting at the reflection in a mirror. In another, she sprinted twenty feet, leaped over a table, grabbed her gun, and then calmly shattered two glass balls that had been tossed in the air as she began her run. Buffalo Bill's "little girl" was a phenomenon.

To top it off, she was also a charmer. As one of her fans recalled, "She was a consummate actress, with a personality that made itself felt as soon as she entered the arena. Even before her name was on the lips of every man, woman and child in America and Europe, the sight of this

The remarkable Miss Oakley fixed a steady gaze on both her targets and her athletic career. *Denver Public Library, Western History Department*

43

BUFFALO BILL'S WILD WEST.
CONGRESS, ROUGH RIDERS OF THE WORLD.

A. Huen & Co., Baltimore, U.S.A.

MISS ANNIE OAKLEY,
THE PEERLESS LADY WING-SHOT.

"When [male competitors in a shooting competition] saw me coming along they laughed at the notion of my shooting against them . . . It kind of galled me to see those hulking chaps so tickled in what was no doubt to them my impertinence in daring to shoot against them—and I reckon I was tickled too when I walked away with the prize."
—ANNIE OAKLEY

Miss Annie Oakley, the Peerless Lady Wing-Shot, was a featured attraction of Buffalo Bill's Wild West when it played London in 1887. *Buffalo Bill Historical Center, Cody, Wyoming, Gift of the Coe Foundation*
FACING PAGE. Guided only by a hand mirror, Annie took unerring aim at targets behind her back. *Buffalo Bill Historical Center, Cody, Wyoming, Vincent Mercaldo Collection*

"Any woman who does not thoroughly enjoy tramping across the country on a clear, frosty morning with a good gun and a pair of dogs does not know how to enjoy life."
—ANNIE OAKLEY, 1901

frail girl among the rough plainsmen seldom failed to inspire enthusiastic plaudits. Her entrance was always a very pretty one. She never walked. She tripped in, bowing, waving, and wafting kisses. Her first few shots brought forth a few screams of fright from the women, but they were soon lost in round after round of applause. It was she who set the audience at ease and prepared it for the continuous crack of firearms which followed." As another observer put it, "Women and children see a harmless woman there, and they do not get worried."

During her sixteen seasons with the show, Annie Oakley became one of the company's biggest box-office draws and, at her peak, is reported to have earned up to $1000 per week (slightly more than the U.S. president). The Sioux chief Sitting Bull adopted her and honored her with the name *Watanya cicilia*, "Little Sure Shot." The New York Ladies Riding Club awarded her a special gold medal to recognize her trickriding skills. When the Wild West travelled to London in 1887, society ladies sought her out to admire the riding costume ("cool, comfortable, and handsome," as one of them described it) that she had designed for her airings in Hyde Park. Edward, the Prince of Wales, asked for her to be presented to him; his wife, Princess Alexandra, celebrated her birthday by sending a gift. Even the queen, roused from her gloomy seclusion in Buckingham Palace, attended a special performance of the show and then called for selected performers, including Miss Oakley, to visit her. "You are a very clever little girl," the queen said approvingly.

These stamps were produced to promote the cowgirls of the Miller Brothers 101 Ranch Real Wild West Show, one of dozens of outfits that eventually followed in Buffalo Bill's footsteps. *Buffalo Bill Historical Center, Cody, Wyoming*

FACING PAGE. Outside the arena, Miss Oakley was the model of middle-class respectability. She is seen here on the grounds of the Chicago World's Fair in 1893. *Buffalo Bill Historical Center, Cody, Wyoming*

National women's buckjumping championships were held in Australia between 1944 and 1958. Among the contestants was a woman who called herself Texas Lil. *Courtesy of Peter N. Poole*

RIGHT. Pioneering buckjumper and showwoman Violet Skuthorpe was pictured in mid-flight on the cover of *The Sydney Mail* in 1935. *National Library of Australia*

THE LADY BUSHRANGER

In Australia, the sport of saddle-bronc riding was born as "buckjumping," and one of its earliest female proponents was a circus entertainer named Jessie Martini. Jessie was born in 1890, the very year that her wealthy father lost his fortune in a financial crash. Because of her family's destitute state and her love of animals, young Jessie was soon apprenticed to a circus where, by 1906, she was appearing as both Jessie Devine, the bareback rider, and Miss Kemp, the self-proclaimed Australian Lady Buckjumping Champion.

In private life, Jessie was also Mrs. Martini, the wife of the circus's owner and male buckjumping specialist. When her husband was killed by his horses in 1907, Jessie took over as proprietor and ringmistress. But then she too was injured in a buckjumping accident, and her new suitor, a Major Hickman, persuaded her to give up the circus and marry him instead. (Under its new ownership, Martini's Circus became "Wild Australia," the antipodean answer to Buffalo Bill's Wild West.)

As events would prove, selling her show was not a prudent move. Hickman soon disappeared and Jessie, now with a young child, was again left destitute. She began to steal and was sent to jail (where her son was taken from her). Once released, she killed a man in self-defence and decided to head for the hills. In the Wollemi Wilderness, she organized a ring of cattle thieves and lived as a fugitive.

Tiring of her outlaw life after several years, she returned to buckjumping, as Miss Kemp, in 1926. Two years later, she was finally brought to trial on a charge of cattle theft and acquitted. Although the long-lost Hickman reappeared in time to pay her bail, she ultimately returned to her mountain hideaway.

The Shufflebottom family, originally from the north of England, toured the country with their Wild West show from the 1890s until the 1960s. Above, the daring Polly (Shufflebottom) Texas serves as a human target for her axe-wielding husband, Jack. *Margaret Shufflebottom Collection, National Fairground Archives, University Library, University of Sheffield*

RIGHT. A doe-eyed cowgirl gazes lovingly at her cowboy hero in this promotional postcard for an English theatrical production

3   YOUNG BUFFALO AND CAROLINE MAY BLANEY

49

Who can say why these handsomely dressed cowpokes are wearing rollerskates? Their portrait was taken at a London photographic studio, perhaps in the 1920s

But if Annie Oakley was clever, she was also very naughty. Respectable Victorian ladies did not make a spectacle of themselves in the show ring. (As one contemporary writer pointed out, A woman is essentially a being of retirement and seclusion, and her nature becomes deteriorated by any employment which brings her before the public.") In performance, she flaunted her body in an unseemly manner—stamping her foot playfully when she missed a target and giving a characteristic little jump-kick as she scampered out of the arena. As a professional sharpshooter, she displayed an unwholesome passion for what many continued to see as a male activity. Worse, she was a career woman long before the phrase had been invented, and one whose husband had willingly reorganized his life in order to help her develop her talents. And, perhaps most alarming of all, she was competitive—constantly training, constantly testing her skills, constantly contesting (and sometimes besting) males in public tournaments. Judged by lace-edged nineteenth-century standards of femininity, Annie Oakley was an outrage.

Yet there she was, petted and preened by the royals and showered with applause from both the public and the press. In part, she earned this praise with her thrilling performances, though athletic skill was no guarantee of public acceptance for a woman. (The only other women who made their living from "sports" at the time were circus acrobats and lady wrestlers, and they were not exactly swamped with calls from Queen Victoria.) But by the 1880s and 1890s, progressive thinkers *were* beginning to approve of moderate physical exercise for young ladies. Provided that sports were undertaken with suitable restraint—so as not to involve any loss of that grace and charm of femininity which when all is said and done is the crown and glory of woman"—then athletics could be encouraged as a preparation for adult life and, especially, for the quintessentially female task of reproduction. After attending a girls' gymnastics class in 1895, one journalist found himself filled with "faith in the future of a country that will be able to draw from so bright-eyed, healthy-bodied, clean-limbed a host, for the mothers of a coming generation." Once married, of course, these rambunctious hosts would be required to put up their hair, lengthen their dresses, cinch their bodies into corsets and conduct themselves with wan refinement.

In the hard light of day, Mrs. Frank Butler was a mature woman on her way to middle age. (Although publicists obligingly took six years off her age when they wrote her promotional

"A girl must, simply because she is a girl, refrain from taking part in healthy recreations. They must not forget they are young ladies."
—UNION STANDARD, WOMEN'S CHRISTIAN TEMPERANCE UNION PAPER, 1890

When Buffalo Bill's show visited Paris in the 1890s, his troupe of "American amazons" was among the most thrilling attractions. *Musée de la Publicité, Paris*

"I don't like bloomers or bloomer women, but I think that sport and healthful exercise make women better, healthier and happier."
—ANNIE OAKLEY, 1897

*"There I was facing the real Wild West, the first white woman to travel with
what society might have considered an impossible outfit."*

—ANNIE OAKLEY

COWGIRLS AND INDIANS

Long before the first ranch woman swung into a man's saddle, Native women had been riding astride on half-wild horses. Many of them were no doubt skilled with firearms as well, quite able to take down a duck or a grouse—or a clay pigeon. Yet Aboriginal women in Wild West shows never enjoyed starring roles as riders or crack shots. At best, they sometimes appeared as anonymous "Indian maidens" or "princesses" in horse races. The rest of the time, they were cast as "squaws," who maintained tipi encampments, rode in processions and, sometimes, helped to torture white captives in "historical" reenactments.

But while Native women were largely prevented from playing cowgirls, white women had considerable freedom to play Natives. Annie Oakley, for example, made the most of her brief friendship with Sitting Bull and was happy to be thought of as his adopted daughter. Lillian Smith, a shooter who had a brief run with Buffalo Bill as "the Girl from California," went on to a career in "brown face" as the Princess Wenona. And Florence Hughes Randolph, who rode as a cowgirl in Wild West productions, circuses, movies and rodeos, also played the starring role in her own show, the exotically titled Princess Mohawk's Wild West Hipprodrome.

Just as cowgirls crossed into territory that was usually assigned to men, they also invaded the space—close to animals and nature—that had been ascribed to "primitives." Thus, while Native women could not easily "go white," a cowgirl could "go Native" whenever she liked.

Wenona, the "Champion Indian Girl Rifle Shot," and Lillian F. Smith, the "California Girl," were one and the same person. *Circus World Museum, Baraboo, Wisconsin/Buffalo Bill Historical Center, Cody, Wyoming*

MISS LILLIAN F. SMITH,
THE "CALIFORNIA GIRL,"
Champion Rifle Shot Of The World.

"What we want to do is give our women even more liberty than they have. Let them do any kind of work that they see fit, and if they do it as well as men, give them the same pay."

—BUFFALO BILL CODY, 1899

COWGIRL FACTS AND FICTIONS

Buffalo Bill focused a loving gaze on the Old West, where rough-riding cowboys trailed cattle across the plains and rugged frontiersmen battled with war-whooping Indians. He invited his audience to watch as he turned the "Page of Passing History" and showed them a wild scene that, by 1890, was already a thing of the past.

Cowgirls didn't fit very well into this nostalgic vision. Although a few women had been present on the cattle drives of the 1870s and 1880s, they had seldom worked as itinerant cowhands (as cowboys generally had). By presenting cowgirls and cowboys as part of the same spectacle, Buffalo Bill created the illusion that "cowboy girls" had been out there in droves, galloping across the country after herds of longhorns. These cowgirls-that-never-were, he implied, were just one more exotic aspect of the great western wilderness that had been subdued by the advance of civilization.

The facts, of course, were very different. Cowgirls were largely products of a New West of family-owned holdings. Between 1875 and 1900, about a quarter of a million American women ran farms and ranches of their own, and millions of others worked alongside their fathers and husbands. Even in 1916, when Buffalo Bill folded his tents for the last time, the real-life, working cowgirl was scarcely on the verge of disappearance.

biography, she had signed on with Cody at age 25 and stayed with the show into her forties.) But in the flickering glow of the carbon arc lights, she became a girl again, free to wear her hair loose, dress in calf-length skirts, and frolic around the ring. Annie Oakley's presentation of herself was a complex performance, as tricky as any of the shooting stunts in her repertoire. Off stage, she played the part of a conventional married woman, who rode sidesaddle, rejected the suffrage movement and kept her hands busy with embroidery between engagements. "To be considered a lady has always been my highest ambition," she said piously. On stage, she appeared as a spunky but appealing child, her strength and sex appeal disguised as cuteness.

And then, of course, she was the girl-star of the Wild West, a context that helped to make perfect sense of her unusual competence. Annie was a hardy prairie flower from the wilds of Kansas. At least, that is the way Buffalo Bill's pitchmen liked to have it. Of course she was keen and courageous—had she not spent her youth trapping wolves, killing bears, catching robbers and standing up to desperate outlaws? If, in plain point of fact, Annie had grown up shooting squirrels and birds in the settled farmlands of Darke County, there was no need to worry about facts. In her turned-up hat, with shotguns ablaze, she was the very picture of a bold western girl.

By the late nineteenth century, the "type," or image, of the spunky American girl had become a popular symbol for the strength and promise of the entire country. "Observers have usually found it possible to write books on the social and economical traits" of a nation "without a parade of petticoats in the headlines," British travel writer James Muirhead noted in 1898. But the writer on the United States found himself "irresistibly compelled" to devote whole chapters to the country's female citizens. The reason, Muirhead suggested, was that American women (especially those from the West) embodied the essential characteristics of the new society: the "intangible quality of Americanism." Thus, Norwegian scholar Hjamar Boyesen—though somewhat alarmed by his encounter with a "pretty western girl" who "had about as much notion of propriety as a cat does of mathematics"—waxed eloquent in his praise for the good nature, generosity, willfulness and pep of American girls in general. French commentator Alexis de Tocqueville approved of their "happy boldness," and his countryman Paul Bourget admired their unprecedented "mixture of feminine delicacy and masculine will." Novelist Henry James painted their portrait as Daisy Miller, that "inscrutable combination of audacity and innocence."

Charming, outdoorsy, independent and determined, The Girl was proof of America's passion for democracy, the product of its dauntless frontier spirit and the promise of bold generations still unborn. In Annie Oakley's performances, this image came energetically to life, in a moving picture of a young country's pride and self-confidence.

FACING PAGE. On a visit to Chicago around 1910, an aging Buffalo Bill posed with some of the young and daring cowgirl performers in his entourage. *Buffalo Bill Historical Center, Cody, Wyoming*

Georgia Duffy, "The Rough Rider From Wyoming," looked every inch the Victorian lady in this promotional portrait from her Wild West days. Her waist has been cinched in through corseting. *American Heritage Center, University of Wyoming*

FACING PAGE. Sometime around 1898, Pawnee Bill Lillie used this poster to advertise a "contest of equine skill," in which "beautiful daring western girls" went up against "Mexican señoritas," including the alluring Miss Rosalia. *Library of Congress/LCUSZ C4-1008*

By the 1890s, criticizing Annie Oakley would have been tantamount to attacking a national icon. She was the first performer to adopt the persona of the all-American cowgirl, and this identification allowed her to earn her living as an athlete and to work in the company of men without being written off as a floozy. She was not "loose" (an accusation that was still commonly thrown at women who publicly engaged in "men's sports"). Nor was she one of the dreadful "new women" who were noisily pressing for education and advancement. Instead, she was a fresh-faced country miss who had come by her skills naturally and honestly in the great work of building a nation. Like the cowboys and Indians with whom she performed in the Wild West shows, she was portrayed as an exotic creation of a distinct phase in the American experience that was now, through the march of progress, receding into the past. What could be more wholesome, and less threatening, than that?

Annie Oakley's success at clearing a space in which she could perform was among the greatest accomplishments of her very accomplished career. "It was uphill work," she admitted, only once, in her private correspondence, "for when I [began] there was a prejudice to live down." Her victory in what she called "the great fight for recognization in the Arena," together with the near-rapture of her fans in the United States, Canada, England, Italy, Germany and France, immediately opened the way for other female performers to join the Wild West. Within a year of Annie Oakley's engagement as the "only white woman" in the cast, Cody had added four more cowgirls to his company. Among the early arrivals was a popular trickrider who billed herself as Emma Lake Hickok, on the grounds that her mother (circus owner Agnes Lake) had married Wild Bill Hickok a few months before his death. But several others—Della Farrell of Colorado and Georgia Duffy, "The Rough Rider from Wyoming"—may actually have been recruited from western ranches. Not only did they ride sidesaddle in decorative dances and drills, but several of them held the spotlight, astride, as bronc riders. "All honor to the American frontier girls who ride so fearlessly!" one pressman enthused.

By 1891, Cody's playbill listed "6 Cowgirls," and a few years later he could boast an entire "Bevy of Beautiful Rancheras, genuine and famous frontier girls" who were guaranteed to thrill with their "feats of daring equestrianism." Rival showman Pawnee Bill Lillie (one of the dozens of producers who were inspired by Cody's success) was tempted to an even more fulsome flood of eloquence. Step right up, his advertisements said, to see "beauteous, dashing, daring and laughing Western girls" who could outride all the other women in the world. Though never more than a highly visible minority in the industry, cowgirls had won a place for themselves in western show business. A few of them were even so bold as to start their own outfits, beginning

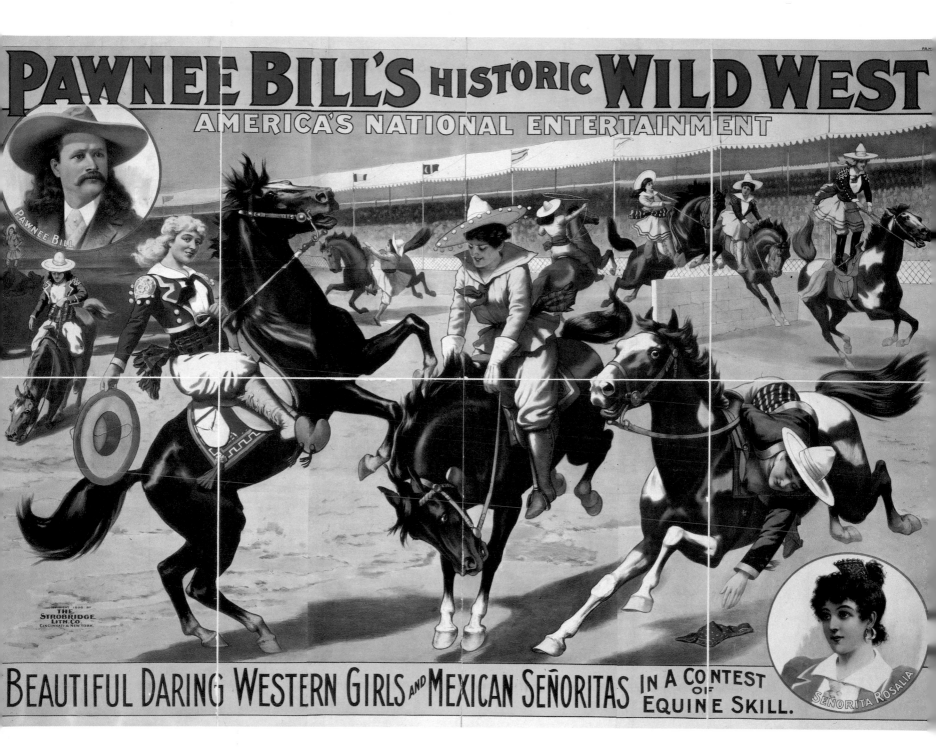

In real life, this soft, seductive-looking cowgirl was a Wild West bronc rider named Lillian Ward. *Buffalo Bill Historical Center, Cody, Wyoming*

FACING PAGE. Cowgirl Jessie Roberts keeps a firm grip on a bronco called Grey Ghost. *Colorado Historical Society*

YOU GOT THE WRONG COWGIRL, BUFFALO BILL

The cowboy of [the 1880s and 1890s] counted physical hardship as a normal part of life's routine . . . Had anyone told him that riding a bucking horse would become a histrionic profession, he would have smiled pityingly. To be sure, Buffalo Bill had started out with his road show, but never could we have been made to believe that it was a forerunner of a national industry.

Once I was besought by one of Buffalo Bill's talent scouts to join his show.

"Me? What on earth could I do?"

"I seen you ride that blue roan outlaw yestidday," he replied, with more admiration than grammar.

"And you saw me keep him *from* bucking, didn't you?"

No, I've never yet let a horse buck with me if I could stop him. I can't see any sense in getting your head all but snapped from your shoulders, your spinal column whipped like a bullwhacker's blacksnake, your insides churned into jelly, even if you stay on, which I usually didn't—not if one could help it! As for making it a profession, that was to laugh!

—Agnes Morley Cleaveland

59

with the Kemp Sisters Wild West in 1896 and the memorably named Luella Forepaugh-Fish company, which was formed in 1903.

Meanwhile, back in Wyoming, a new form of western entertainment was being introduced to the public. Cheyenne Frontier Days, "the Daddy of 'Em All," made its debut in 1897 and quickly set the pattern for big-time rodeo. In drawing up the program of events, organizers took their inspiration from two established traditions. On the one hand, they looked back to the informal games that had always been a feature of ranch society—horseback races, calf riding, bronc busting—friendly sports in which women and girls had often taken part. (Rodeo cowgirl Goldie St. Clair remembered getting her start by riding rank horses in a wheat field, for the entertainment of her neighbors.) On the other hand, the new show took its cue from the exhibitions of bronc riding, steer roping and general Cowboy Fun that had long been standard fare in the Wild West arena. Here too cowgirls had won their spurs as participants. Yet Frontier Days was launched without a single event for female competitors.

The reasons for this exclusion were hinted at in 1899, when a Ladies' Cow Pony Race was belatedly added to the festivities. Although contestants were required to ride astride like tough Wyoming girls should, the winner was given a sidesaddle. Apparently, officials had some misgivings about rough-and-tumble athletics for women. But the contestants and the audience seem not to have been fussed by similar worries. "Nowhere else in the world do women display the fearless horsemanship to be found on the prairies of Wyoming, and as the ladies came under the

wire at break neck speed they were wildly cheered," the local paper exulted; "interest taken in the race was greater than [in] any of the [other] running events of the afternoon."

By 1902, a number of ranch women were badgering officials for an opportunity to compete as bronc riders, but the worthy gentlemen could not be moved. Finally, in 1904—almost twenty years after the first woman had climbed on a bucking horse in Buffalo Bill's Wild West—a cow-girl quietly took matters into her own hands. A young ranch owner from Colorado named Bertha Kapernick entered herself in both the bronc-riding contest and the wild horse race. Because no one had ever expected women to participate in these events, the rulebook failed to say in so many words that they couldn't. Although Kapernick did not win either competition, she did steal the hearts of the audience. One day, when the cowboys were forced off the field by a downpour of rain, Miss Kapernick was called back to entertain the restless crowd with an exhibition of her bronc-riding prowess. The bronc in question was a "long lanky roan, full of deviltry" and, despite the mud, Kapernick rode him to submission. "It was one of the most remarkable exhibitions of rough riding ever seen here," the paper reported, "and would have been exciting had the rider been a man. As it was, the great multitude cheered . . . this extraordinary young lady who has conquered the west." Not only were the cowboys shamed into continuing their performance, but Frontier Days was persuaded to add ladies' bronc riding to its program in 1906.

When the Pendleton Roundup was founded a few years later, Kapernick was on hand under her new name of Bertha Blancett (like many rodeo women, she had married a cowboy). One of

Dozens of women participated in the second annual Pendleton Roundup in 1911, some as athletes and others as "queen" contestants. *Umatilla County Historical Society*

Cowgirls Florence La Due (top) and Bertha Blancett were both proclaimed champions at the first Calgary Stampede, held in 1912. *Glenbow Archives, Calgary, Alberta, NA1029-19 and NA335-18*

FACING PAGE. Early rodeo cowgirls were well treated by the press, which reported on their events in admiring detail. Even competitors who lost (like Hazel Walker) were sometimes praised for their gumption. *Glenbow Archives, Calgary, Alberta, NA335-26*

the new show's most versatile stars, she soon came within a few points of winning the coveted title of All Round Cowboy. But the best showcase for her talents, and those of other cowgirl performers, was the first ever Calgary Stampede of 1912. With a total purse of $20,000 in gold and a promotional blitz that spanned the continent, the Stampede was the richest and most ballyhooed contest in the history of ranch sports. Envisaged by its director, western entertainer Guy Weadick, as a world-class *cowboy* contest with all the glitz and glamor of a Wild West show, the program nonetheless included a varied slate of competitions for women, including saddle-bronc riding, trickriding, fancy roping and a relay race in which riders had to pelt around the course, vault to the ground, saddle up a new mount and scream down the track once more. Thrills and spills galore.

Perhaps Weadick the Showman made so much room for the women because he knew they were crowd pleasers; or maybe it was Weadick the Husband who decided to feature them. His wife and vaudeville partner was a cowgirl trickrider and fancy roper who performed under the glamorous name of Florence, or Flores, La Due. Born plain Grace Maud Bensell in plain old Minnesota, she was the only daughter of a wealthy lawyer and judge. And had she not been, as she put it, a bit of a "boy," she might have settled sweetly into upper-class life. But "I wanted to ride," she remembered, "so I started when I was four. They said a rider had to clean out the stables. So I did." In time, she wanted to join a Wild West show, and to perform with Will Rogers, and to ride a bucking horse on a vaudeville stage; and so she did all those things, as well. Now, perhaps, she wanted a chance to test her skill in public competition against an elite field.

Joining La Due and Blancett in Calgary's superstar lineup was the most famous cowgirl of the day, a veteran performer of theaters, conventions, rodeos and fairs named Lucille Mulhall. The perfect hybrid of ranch hand, debutante and showgirl, Lucille had spent her childhood summers on her family's ranch, her winters at boarding school and her adolescence as the headline performer in her father's Wild West productions. Billed as the "Champion Lady Rider and Roper of the World," she was promoted as "America's First Cowgirl," and many people believed that the word "cowgirl" had been coined especially to describe her. If, in fact, she missed out on those honors by a couple of decades or more, she nonetheless deserved recognition as an all-round athlete and entertainer. At Calgary, she narrowly lost the roping competition to Miss La Due, who dazzled the judges by, among other feats, tying a man hand and foot in three quick flicks of her loop.

HAZEL WALKER THROWN BY "BUTTONS", "BUT SHE RODE HIM JUST THE SAME",
"THE STAMPEDE", CALGARY ALTA 1912   OFFICIAL PHOTO No 5
MARCELL

63

COWGIRL RACE, THE ROUNDUP, LET'ER BUCK, PENDLETON, OREGON. W-107.

But Lucille Mulhall did get into the headlines with another of her specialties. She was one of relatively few women who roped and hog-tied steers, and the only one to enter the "cowboy steer roping" at the Stampede. Exactly why Mulhall was permitted to risk herself in this hazardous event—which involved a hand-to-hoof contest with half a ton of beef—is a bit of a mystery, since another cowgirl had been discouraged from entering the much-more-sedate wild horse race. (In Guy Weadick's opinion, the race was "rough enough for the men let alone the ladies.") Maybe Lucille's reputation as an "Amazon" had preceded her. At 18, in 1904, she was reported to have roped, dropped and tied three steers in little more than 2 minutes—and to have claimed a grand prize of $10,000. At 26, in 1912, she was not so fortunate; but the following year, at Weadick's one-and-only Winnipeg Stampede, she won the first two rounds of competition and, though eventually defeated,

LUCILLE MULHALL CHAMPION LADY STEER ROPER OF THE WORLD. WINNIPEG STAMPEDE 1913. PHOTO 42. © CAN-U.S.A MARCELL OF CALGARY. TIME - 33⅘ SEC.

was lauded and applauded as the Champion Lady Steer Roper of the World.

Another Winnipeg cowgirl surpassed even Mulhall's accomplishment. Tillie Baldwin (a newcomer to the scene in 1913) participated in the women's relay, won the ladies' trickriding and outclassed a field of men in the standing Roman race. In this demanding contest, the riders thundered around a half-mile track aboard two horses, with one foot firmly planted on each heaving back. Heats were run daily during the Stampede, and the competitor with the best average time was declared the winner. As the *Winnipeg Tribune* told the story, Tillie "drove her twin mounts at a gait which would frighten many men . . . to death." And her flat-out run was not the cowgirl's only daring performance. She turned up for all her competitions wearing pants. To be more accurate, she wore bloomers, similar to the ones she had used for gymnastics in her Norwegian girlhood. Thus sensibly attired, she had dazzled the judges with headstands and other new trickriding stunts, and had evened the odds with the cowboys in the Roman race. What's more, she had entered herself in the he-man event of bulldogging, or steer wrestling.

Even as a steer roper, Lucille Mulhall dressed decorously, in a hair ribbon, white blouse and bulky split skirt. Would she have been even faster if she'd worn pants? *Glenbow Archives, Calgary, Alberta, NA1029-27*

FACING PAGE. A field of women riders thunders around the bend during an early running of the Pendleton Roundup. *Wesley Andrews photo, Oregon Historical Society OrHi17200*

RECOLLECTIONS OF A LADY BRONC RIDER

I lived when I wanted to, the way I wanted to, and that is saying a lot for one mortal. I was born March 27, 1887 on a horse ranch at the foot of Bear Tooth Mountain north of Helena, Montana, and if there is a horse in the zodiac then I am sure I must have been born under its sign, for the horse has shaped and determined my whole way of life.

Perhaps it is odd that a woman should be born with an all-consuming love of horseflesh, but I have never thought so. It seems to me as normal as breathing air or drinking water, that the biggest thing on my horizon has been the four-legged critter with mane and tail.

If there are not horses in heaven, I do not want to go there. But I believe there will be . . . , for God loved them or He would not have created them with such majesty . . . How can I explain to dainty, delicate women what it is like to climb down into a rodeo chute onto the back of a wild horse? How can I tell them it is a challenge that lies deep in the bones—a challenge that may go back to prehistoric man and his desire to conquer the outlaw and the wilderness? . . .

Now that I am what young people consider an old woman, and I look back at my life, I can truthfully say that if I had it all to do over again, I would live it exactly the same. From such a statement you gather that I have liked it. I have *loved* it, every single, wonderful, suffering, exhilarating, damned, blessed moment of it. And if, with my present arthritis, I must pay the price of every bronco ride that I have ever made, then I pay for it gladly. Pain is not too great a price to pay for the freedom of the saddle and a horse between the legs.

—Fanny Sperry Steele, Lady Bucking Horse Champion of the World for 1912 and 1913, 1976

FACING PAGE. Kitty Canutt (left), Prairie Rose Henderson and Ruth Roach were bronc riders and good friends, 1916. *Wyoming Division of Cultural Resources*

66

PRAIRIE ROSE
KITTIE CANUTT   RUTH ROACH
PENDLETON ROUND UP
(DOUBLEDAY)

NATURAL CHILDBIRTH

For decades, women had been advised to avoid vigorous sport because they were likely to damage their reproductive organs. But in 1937 one articulate cowgirl answered this argument.

A cow-woman takes no coddling, gets no martyr complex just because she is going to have a baby. She rides in the show up until two months before she expects the child—and she is back in the saddle bronc-riding in contests not later than six weeks afterward. This is the reward of developing strong backs, erect posture, educated muscles.

A cowgirl would no more think of wearing spike heels, a tight girdle, a binding brassiere, than she would drink poison. It is not that a cowgirl does not want to attract the masculine eyes, but we know cowboys. They like slimness, line, grace—but they want it natural.

Women with curved spines and swayed abdomens, with half the muscles in their bodies wasted from lack of exercise and use, who fear childbirth because they have not kept their bodies natural, wonder why their lives are not rich, full, vital—yet they never dream that the violation of natural health laws is the cause of everything.

—Bronc rider Alice Greenough, *Physical Culture* magazine, 1937

67

"Kitty Canutt"
Champion Lady Rider
of the World,
on
Winnemucca

#10.

Copyright 1919 by
H. J. Rogner,
Rawlins, Wyo.

VERA McGINNIS
IN THE DRUNKEN RIDE
THE ROUND-UP, PENDLETON, ORE. ©W.S.Bo

"I was born in Texas where they don't raise sissies. I've never been afraid of any- thing in my life except a rattlesnake."
—LEO RODMAN,
RODEO AND WILD WEST COWGIRL

Daredevil cowgirl Vera McGinnis careens down the course at a gallop in a trickriding event called the Drunken Ride. Races of various sorts were popular features of early rodeos, and cowgirls often doubled as jockeys and relay riders. *Oregon Historical Society OrHi27430*

FACING PAGE. Kitty Canutt sits tall in the saddle at a rodeo in Rawlins, Wyoming in 1919. *Library of Congress/LCUSZ62-99834*

OVERLEAF. Billed as the "Woman World Champion Bucking Horse, Trick and Fancy Rider," Tillie Baldwin began her adult life as a hairdresser. A self-made rodeo cowgirl, she expanded her repertoire of riding stunts by dressing like a gymnast. *Glenbow Archives, Calgary, Alberta, NA446-107/Oregon Historical Society OrHi21046*

Bulldogging was a down-and-dirty sport, in which the contestant leaped from a running horse onto the back of a steer, grabbed its horns, and attempted to bring it down by wrenching its neck. (The event was eventually outlawed because steers were sometimes killed.) Not sur-prisingly, perhaps, other cowgirls were slow to follow on Baldwin's pioneering appearance as a steer wrestler. (Indeed, the next female bulldogger to make a name for herself was Eloise "Fox" Hastings, and she didn't come onto the scene for another decade.) What may be more surpris-ing is that cowgirls were also slow to imitate Baldwin's other innovation. Despite the obvious

advantages of trousers, most cowgirls continued to outfit themselves in long, bulky split skirts, which were both a nuisance and a hazard. Lucille Mulhall, for one, knew what it meant to be dragged beneath her horse when the heavy fabric of her skirt got caught in a stirrup. Yet, though they sometimes gathered their hems with elastic for trickriding, cowgirls did not routinely wear pants until the mid-1920s.

In a reminiscence published in 1931, Will Rogers praised Lucille Mulhall for her decorous clothing. "Lucille never dressed like the Cowgirl you know today," he assured his readers, "no loud colors, no short leather skirts and great big hat, no sir, her skirt was divided, but long, away down over her patent leather boot tops, a whipcord grey, or grey broadcloth, small stiff-brim hat and always a white silk shirtwaist.

"There was a lot of class to the Mulhall outfit, none of your cheap show stuff." Indeed, class—or ladylike graces—had always been part of the cowgirl package. A gal could be tough and competitive, but she'd sure better look like a gal. By the turn of the century, this rule had been given new force by the findings of social science. In a study of *The Female Offender* published in 1895, a well-regarded scholar named Cesare Lombroso had conclusively shown that women who looked and acted like males were probably congenital criminals. And the new discipline of sexology, as practiced by Richard von Krafft-Ebing and Havelock Ellis, had concluded that women with masculine tastes were "sexual inverts," or lesbians. Passionate friendships between women, which formerly had been interpreted as a natural aspect of female experience, had now been scientifically defined as a perversion. Among the diagnostic symptoms of this "abnormality" were a desire to wear trousers, an interest in male sports and an ambition to compete against, and defeat, men.

In 1929, cowgirls Reine Shelton (left), Fox Hastings and trickrider *extraordinaire* Tad Lucas entertained themselves at the Hotel Sherman in Chicago, as they awaited the opening of a major rodeo. *Library of Congress/LCUSZ62-73633*

FACING PAGE. Fox Hastings became famous in the twenties and thirties as a steer wrestler. Her fastest time was 17 seconds, a record she set in 1924. *Wyoming Division of Cultural Resources*

"To the rodeo crowd she is Fox Hastings, cowgirl extraordinary. To neighbors she is Mrs. Mike Hastings, a good cook and tidy housekeeper."
—NEWSPAPER STORY

Cowgirl Cuties

This year's crop of rodeo cowgirls sets a new high standard of good looks and it takes more than an outlaw bronc to make one of the cuties forget her mascara.

Tough as any ranch hand when it comes to riding, the girls spend as much time on their makeup as any chorine in Rainbeau Garden. One rides with a fresh gardenia over one ear, and they all touch up with perfume.

Their tack rooms in the rodeo barns back of the Coliseum are fully equipped with mirrors. No cowgirl would think of coming out in the arena without powder, rouge, lipstick, eyeshadow and mascara.

Their costumes are practical, but ultra feminine. Most of the girls who sew as well as they ride broncs, make their own . . . The cowgirl costumes, braided and embroidered and worn with bright blouses, are all made of pastel flannels and tailored—the girls hope—to stand up under the toughest wear. That's quite a trick of tailoring, considering the way the clothes fit. You may have noticed what happened to the breeches of a cowgirl trick rider Monday afternoon.

She was very embarrassed.

—Bess Stephenson, *Fort Worth Star-Telegram*

To perform in big-city rodeos, the cowgirls of the twenties decked themselves out in lustrous shirts, flowing sashes and artfully draped bandanas. From left to right in the front row are Fox Hastings, Ruth Roach and Florence Randolph. Back row: an unidentified cowgirl, Bea Kirnan, another unidentified cowgirl and Mabel Strickland. *Wyoming Division of Cultural Resources*

FAR LEFT. Vera McGinnis claimed to have been the first woman to wear pants in the rodeo arena. She designed this Spanish-influenced outfit for a rodeo at Wembley Stadium in London in 1924. *National Cowgirl Hall of Fame and Western Heritage Center*

FACING PAGE. Prairie Rose Henderson created this
flamboyant costume in about 1910. *American Heritage
Center, University of Wyoming*

Alice Greenough, below, grew up breaking wild mus-
tangs in Montana for her father, "Packsaddle Ben"
Greenough. In later life, she made a career of riding
rank horses at the rodeo and even made occasional out-
ings as a bullrider. But she still enjoyed feminine
touches like nail polish and a flower at her throat.
Montana Historical Society

If it had taken scientists to define this new "disorder," it didn't take an expert to see that cowgirls fit all too neatly into its categories. Indeed, a slang term that was sometimes applied to black
lesbians was "bull dagger" (a corruption of "bulldogger," or steer wrestler). If lesbians could be
seen as cowgirls, might not cowgirls also be lesbians? As a matter of simple statistics, there must
certainly have been homosexual and bisexual women in western sports and show business. After
all, by 1916, no fewer than 240 women were competing in pro rodeo and performing as cowgirls
in Wild West shows, a large enough group to include a normal range of sexual interests. But the
lesbian women, whoever they were, stayed in deep hiding, their love affairs camouflaged by het-
erosexual marriages and their supposedly "mannish" inclinations disclaimed with cowgirl charm.

For most cowgirls, lesbian or straight, maintaining a few feminine touches was not a painful
masquerade. "I know you think I'm a paradox," champion cowgirl Mabel Strickland once told
a New York reporter, "but I belong in the saddle for I've been there since I was three. I love the
open, dogs, horses, a gun, the trees, flowers . . . Still I love dresses and everything that goes with
them." If it was prudent for a female athlete to keep up her sex appeal, it could also be good fun.
Since rodeo clothing for women was seldom sold in the stores, most professional cowgirls
designed and made their own. A performer like Prairie Rose Henderson—who once showed up
to compete in boots, silk stockings, bloomers and a skirt trimmed with ostrich plumes—could
become as famous for her clothes as for her bronc riding. By experimenting with a wide range
of fabrics and styles that expressed their "feminine" side, rodeo cowgirls created a vogue for
fancy western garments that is still very much alive.

But no matter how hard they tried, rodeo cowgirls couldn't quite get it right. Had they
refused to act feminine, they would have been outcasts. By happily agreeing to do so, they marked
themselves as specialty acts. In 1924, when a group of women (Fox Hastings, Prairie Rose
Henderson, Mabel Strickland and Lorena Trickey) asked to enter the men-only events at
Pendleton, and thereby get into the official running for the All Round Cowboy award, their
request was promptly turned down. Cowgirls were not cowboys. It was only natural that women
should have fewer opportunities to compete. It was only natural that they should compete for
smaller purses than the guys.

And the fact was, it *was* only natural for the times. In the big wide world outside the rodeo
arena, women were just achieving the right to vote in the teens and early twenties. Those few
who worked outside the home earned only half as much as their male colleagues. (Indeed, some
cowgirls were attracted to rodeo partly because the pay was better than in "women's" jobs, such
as waiting tables or clerking in stores.) In sports, athletes like Channel swimmer Gertrude Ederle

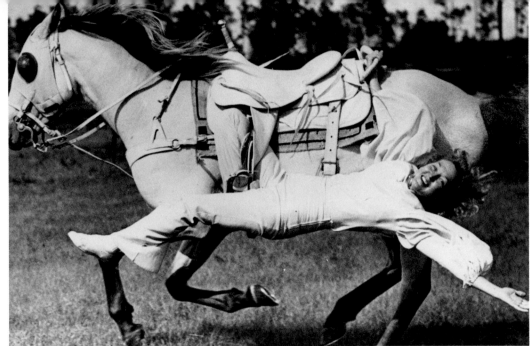

Ride 'Em, Cowgirl

And then Ruth Roach went out on Roaney. The little horse was very fresh, but she sat him like a rock. The bronk bounced and snorted and plunged against the wire, driving the near on-lookers aloft, hanging to the meshes by their hands. From this elevated point of view they looked down on horse and rider bucketing below. There were roars of laughter and the cry "That just beats it!" As the horse swung round and round and would not leave the wire. A circling dust cloud followed him; Ruth Roach's shirt came out of her belt and her hair tossed up and down under her hat but her bridle hand was raised above the saddle horn and her other waved in the air. One more strenuous plunge, and the horse came to a stand. She threw an arm round the waist of the hazer who pulled her from the saddle. Then she raised a hand in quick salute, acknowledging the clapping, and ran flushed with exertion to her friends. "My God, Ruth, but you've had a ride!"

—Charles Simpson, *El Rodeo,* 1925

Trickrider Faye Blackstone, above, invented this move, which she called the "reverse fender drag." *National Cowgirl Hall of Fame and Western Heritage Center*

LEFT. Rodeo cowgirl Bonnie Gray supplemented her income by jumping over automobiles. On her wedding day, she and King Tut leaped over a car in which her groom and maid of honor were seated. *American Heritage Center, University of Wyoming*

and tennis player Helen Wills were only beginning to make their presence felt in a realm that was dominated by male superstars such as Jack Dempsey and Babe Ruth. But in the rodeo arena, female performers had already found a prominent place for themselves. Whatever disadvantages they may have suffered relative to the men (and whatever their inability to address their problems), cowgirls were nonetheless the first significant group of professional women athletes in North America and the first to be taken seriously by the public and the press.

From Annie Oakley onwards, few cowgirls had ever declared themselves to be feminists. Lucille Mulhall probably spoke for most when she expressed cold disinterest in the subject. In the view of most women's suffragists, women were moral and pure, the natural opponents of evils such as promiscuity and booze. Rodeo and Wild West cowgirls—many of whom were much-married and knew how to enjoy a drink—represented altogether earthier interests. They were not intellectuals or middle-class church ladies, who strove to articulate worthy ideals in well-rounded sentences. They were entertainers, and their message, if they had one, was expressed in their performances.

As the market for rodeo expanded in the twenties, cowgirls took their daring body language to new audiences in big cities: St. Louis, Philadelphia, Los Angeles, Chicago, Boston, New York—even London, England. (From 1922 on, Madison Square Garden in New York was rodeo's premiere venue for almost four decades.) Just as they had always done out West, the cowgirls, quite naturally, presented themselves to the press as pleasant young women. "We went behind the scenes expecting to interview half a dozen tomboys," a reporter for the *New York Times* confessed, "but found ourselves in the presence of six mistresses of dignified deportment." But when the crowd thronged the hall and the spotlights were on, the image the cowgirls projected was less decorous. Maidenly dignity would have to look after itself when there were bucking broncs to conquer, steers to wrestle and "suicide drags" to perform. Nice girls, the cowgirls' performances said, were tough and courageous. Nice girls could get physical.

To the other "nice girls" watching from the cheap seats at Madison Square Garden, these performances must have been buzzing with excitement. A new generation of young women, they too were bucking convention, by bobbing their hair, shortening their hems and (horrors!) using slang. Like the cowgirls, they were playful and zestful and, to a prudent elder, could seem careless, as they danced through the night at public ballrooms or went "rubbering" about the streets to look for men. As journalist Hutchins Hapgood put it in 1910, the young working women of East Side New York shared the adventurous character of "a rather wild young man." When the cowgirls went for the gusto, these young fans knew what they meant. Let her buck? You'd better believe it.

HT, WINNER
MPIONSHIP
O BUSTING
EYENNE, WYO.
7,
HION PARK
. AUG. 4,
THIS PICTURE
M.
© 1917, D.F. PHOTO, CO, IN

MABEL STRICKLAND
Champion Cowgirl

"I can honestly say the glamor never
faded. It dimmed once in a while when
I was hurt or overworked, but after a rest
I always felt I wouldn't trade being a
rodeo cowgirl for any other profession."
—VERA McGINNIS

Mabel Strickland, "Champion Cowgirl," won recognition in relay racing, trickriding and steer roping. In the early twenties, she was awarded the McAlpin Trophy as the all-round cowgirl at Cheyenne Frontier Days. A noted "beauty," she was crowned queen of the Pendleton Roundup in 1927. *American Heritage Center, University of Wyoming*

OVERLEAF. A resplendent Dale Evans leans against the gate of a studio "corral." On the right, Dale clings to Trigger, as Roy Rogers looks on in mock alarm. *Photofest (with thanks to the Roy Rogers and Dale Evans Museum, Victorville, California)*

RHINESTONE COWGIRLS

Dale Evans made a cowgirl out of me.

from *Thank Heavens for Dale Evans*, an album by the Dixie Chicks, 1990

The earliest cowgirl adventure stories were told in dime novels and magazines like *Rough Rider Weekly*. The caption beneath this illustration reads: "She had snatched the blacksnake from Old Dennis as she passed the grub-wagon. Now she laid it into the stampeding herd with vicious strokes. Would she turn them in time?" *Denver Public Library, Western History Department*

FACING PAGE. In 1902, Annie Oakley trod the boards as Nance Berry, the title role in a spirited melodrama called *The Western Girl*. The play included shooting demonstrations and the appearance on stage of a horse-drawn stagecoach. *Buffalo Bill Historical Center, Cody, Wyoming*

efore the cowgirls first wowed the crowds at Madison Square Garden, another western performer was strutting her stuff for New York audiences. Her name was Mary Louise Cecilia Guinan—better known as "Texas"—and she had her own unique take on the cowgirl virtues of glamor and guts. Born on a ranch near Waco in 1884, she proudly declared herself the equal of any "tobacco-chewin' cowpoke" when it came to riding, shooting, roping steers and twirling a lariat. Indeed, as a young woman she occasionally competed in small-time rodeos and even signed on briefly with a second-rate Wild West show. But Miss Guinan was too ambitious to settle for anything lackluster, so armed with her diploma from the American Conservatory of Music, she had headed for New York and what she envisaged as a brilliant career on Broadway.

More than a decade later, in 1917, she found herself on the wrong side of thirty and still scrambling for jobs as a hoofer. "We poor chorus girls were always looking for some new stunt whereby to distinguished ourselves," she later recalled, and this time Texas knew she had to come up with a show-stopper. "When I asked the manager if I might ride a horse down the runway instead of merely dancing down, he said, 'All right, if you don't kill too many customers.'" So out came Texas dolled up in black-lace chaps, mounted on a snow-white horse and spinning her lariat. The audience dived for cover as she thundered down the ramp, but at least one observer was impressed by her act. "After the show a movie man signed me up [for] a two-reel western . . . and what a time I had!"

From the beginning, the American motion-picture industry had looked to the West, and western show business, for some of its most distinctive images. In the 1890s, when Thomas Edison produced the first commercial "movies" (flickering ninety-second films that were exhibited in peep-show machines), he had called on his friend Bill Cody and a troupe of Native performers from the Wild West show to be among his first subjects. A few weeks later, the famous Miss Annie Oakley visited his studio to demonstrate her spectacular rapid-fire shooting. To

RUTH MIX AT FLA COW CAPITAL ROUND-UP KISSIMMEE (DOUBLEDAY) MIX

Edison's satisfaction, his new camera caught all the action, from the smoke puffing out of her rifle to the shattering of her glass balls.

Film was the up-and-coming popular entertainment, and had she been a little younger Annie Oakley would no doubt have been part of it. She might, for example, have recreated the role of Nance Berry, the hard-riding, straight-shooting western girl whom she once portrayed in the theater. Nance would have cut a fine figure on the silver screen, as she foiled all the dastardly villains and won the heart of the handsome Lieutenant Hawley. Or Oakley could have stood before the camera as Dell Dauntless of the Double D Ranch, the dashing-and-womanly hero of a dime-novel western series. In the minds of her admirers, Dell was "Class A among Western girls," and she would surely have been a hit with movie-goers as well.

Sadly, neither Dell, nor Nance, nor Annie herself made it to Hollywood, but other cowgirl performers eagerly crossed over into the new medium. Lucille Mulhall is said to have earned a million dollars by performing in silent films, and less-famous performers picked up spare cash by working as extras. For walking or riding through western scenes (often in sunbonnets and skirts), they received a few dollars a day and, at noon, a nice box lunch. "It was like being on a picnic," as one of them put it. Even rodeo champions like Bertha Blancett, Mabel Strickland and Vera McGinnis spent the off-season in the movie business, working as horse wranglers or stunt-women. "I remember doubling for a star on the Beverly Hills bridle path one day," McGinnis recalled, "and doing five falls off a cantering horse for ten bucks a fall." It was a hard and poorly paid job. "But, I was glad to get the work; my only complaint was there wasn't enough of it."

Most of the action in silent westerns was reserved for the men, especially for cowboy heroes such as Hoot Gibson, Tom Mix and Bronco Billy Anderson. But, surprisingly often, pictures came along that offered considerable scope to cowgirl performers as well. A film called *Western Girls*, made in 1912, featured two sisters who dressed up in cowboy clothes, caught a gang of robbers and delivered them at gunpoint to the sheriff. Three years later, Wild West cowgirl Helen Gibson took on the starring role in *The Hazards of Helen*, a long-running serial in which a "girl telegrapher" kept the railroad running with her quick wits and bold deeds. Another cliffhanger from the same era, a twenty-five-part series called *The Girl from Frisco*, cast a ranch-girl-turned-actress named Marin Sais as ranch-girl-turned-amateur-detective Barbara Brent.

The Hazards of Helen ran to 119 heart-stopping episodes, with the title role shared between a stunt-woman and actress named Helen Holmes and a rodeo cowgirl named Helen Gibson. *American Museum of the Moving Image, Gift of William R. Bogert, Jr.*

FACING PAGE. Ruth Mix, daughter of silent-movie star Tom Mix, appeared in several films, including a 1935 short entitled *Fighting Pioneers* in which she starred as Wenona, the war chief of the Crows. *Wyoming Division of Cultural Resources*

Marin Sais, top, abandoned her youthful desire to sing grand opera and instead became an action heroine in Hollywood. She played her first western role in 1911 and her last in 1953. *Academy of Motion Picture Arts and Sciences*

BOTTOM. Like a number of other rodeo cowgirls, Vera McGinnis looked to the movies for excitement, glamor and much-needed cash. *National Cowgirl Hall of Fame and Western Heritage Center*

FACING PAGE. Dorothy Gish played a gun-slinging gal faced with comic complications in a 1919 movie called *Nugget Nell. Photofest*

Before long, Sais went on to create a second cowgirl heroine, Madge King, in a chapter-play called *The American Girl*. In one typical episode, Madge chased the villain on horseback and captured him with her lasso; in another, she stood up to the bad guy in a gun duel.

When Texas Guinan made her movie debut in 1917, she set her sights on being the toughest of the tough-girl heroines. Her argument was straightforward. Women had helped to conquer the West; why shouldn't they now be allowed to conquer the western? At first, her producers demurred—fans might not like a masterful female who could meet force with force. But Texas held her ground. Exchanging her black-lace chaps for a gunbelt and man-style pants, she was soon the star of several dozen western-action films with titles like *Get-Away Kate* (1917), *The Gun Woman* (1918), *The She Wolf* (1919), *The Girl Sheriff* and *I Am the Woman* (both 1921). Well-promoted by her studios and well-received by exhibitors, Texas was touted as something totally new and promising in the history of the cinema. As one of her producers had it, "The ingenue, sweet and bewitching, will always be with us, but the day of the woman of brawn and brains is about to break upon the horizon."

Texas Guinan was the undisputed hero of her films, a straight-shooting gunslinger with "a punch in her gauntlet and a snap in her rawhide whip." And yet, as her promoters were at pains to assert, she still "possessed all the graces and charms of a woman." No ladylike "little missie" à la Annie Oakley, Texas was nonetheless sometimes constrained by the demands of womanhood. In a film called *Little Miss Deputy*, produced in 1919, she faced a choice between her duties as a hero and as a woman when, as deputy sheriff, she was to hang the man she loved. As a "lawman," she has no option but to get on with the job; but for a woman to renounce love would be intolerable. Inevitably, in the closing scenes, Texas proves that her man has been framed and—ever the hero—can stand by his side as the credits roll.

In any real-life contest between love and ambition, Texas always saw to it that ambition won. By 1921, she had divorced her third husband, walked away from her fifth film producer and formed her own film company, Texas Guinan Productions. "I got twelve real cowboys, a scenario writer [Mildred Sledge], a cameraman, a carload of cartridges, my horse 'Waco' from Texas, and went to work. We made a picture a week." In all, she claimed to have made more than 300 movies and to have done all her stunt work herself. "We never changed plots," she admitted, "only the horses." But audiences didn't seem to mind, and her films played in movie houses around the world.

But if there was money to be made as a movie cowgirl, there was more of it back in New York. By 1924, Texas had unbuckled the guns from her curvaceous hips and squirmed into an

evening gown. For the better part of the next decade she would flourish as the queen of New York speakeasies, shouting out her trademark greeting, "Hello, sucker!" and closing every show with an exhortation to give "the little girls" in her chorus line "a great big hand." If her film persona had leaned towards the masculine, she now indulged in an extravagant evocation of everything feminine—a kind of female, female impersonation that was later amplified and developed by Mae West.

Texas's film heroics, on the other hand, did not attract imitators. Perhaps no one had the gall to follow in her footsteps. Or perhaps developments in the film industry had by now made it too difficult for women to break in. In the good old days, when Texas got her start, film making had been a wide-open activity, with plenty of scope for independent productions and female initiative. Before 1920, a majority of the scriptwriters, film editors and star performers in American film had been women. More women worked as directors, cinematographers and producers than has ever been the case since. By the mid-twenties, the big studios had asserted their control of the film industry, and women were systematically excluded from creative and executive roles. The Big Boys weren't interested in female action heroes, and it would be twenty years or more before such characters began, ever so sporadically, to reappear in westerns. Instead, women were cast as damsels in distress, for the hero to rescue, and dewy-eyed maidens, for him to kiss.

Meanwhile, cowgirls in the rodeo were in for a rough ride as well. Two events in 1929 marked the beginning of the end for their "privileged" participation in professional sport. The first was the death that year, at the Pendleton Roundup, of a popular bronc-riding champion named Bonnie McCarroll. A seventeen-year veteran of the rodeo circuit, McCarroll got

"She came out of the vast unknown regions of the West with the spirit of the desert and the power and the brawn of those compelled to defend their own by force of might and will—and yet she possessed all the graces and charms of a woman."
—ADVERTISEMENT FOR TEXAS GUINAN'S FILMS, 1919

LEFT. Texas Guinan commanded the center of the action in her silent films, many of which she produced herself. *Academy of Motion Picture Arts and Sciences*

93

Some female bronc riders rode "slick" like the men (with their stirrups hanging loose). But women were also permitted to perform with their stirrups "hobbled" (tied together under the horse), because this was thought to make their ride easier. Riding slick in 1915, Bonnie McCarroll was thrown clear of her horse (above). Riding hobbled in 1929, she got caught in her gear and was killed.

Denver Public Library, Western History Department

"After 1941 the girls were contracted [to perform at Madison Square Garden]. They called us glamor girls or something and they hired us for color. We rode barrels and rode in the grand entry. And we were paid to do it. I thought it was real silly. I liked the bronc riding."

—FERN SAWYER,
RODEO COWGIRL

hung up in her stirrups and was trampled during what was to have been her last competition. Although she was not the first woman (much less the first person) to die in the rodeo ring, the response to her misfortune was extraordinary. Women's bronc riding was immediately scratched from the program at Pendleton. By 1941, the event would be banned from all major competitions, including the world championship at Madison Square Garden. With the frontier days long past, the ladies now needed protection, it seemed, even from themselves.

The other bad news for rodeo cowgirls in 1929 was the formation, by a group of rodeo producers, of the Rodeo Association of America. In an attempt to standardize the sport, the RAA soon offered official accreditation to rodeos that included a specified list of four, and later eight, events. None of the rodeo producers were female and, not surprisingly, none of the designated contests were open to women. The result was that women's events were gradually squeezed off rodeo programs. An association of rodeo performers, formed in 1936, might have resisted this trend, except that it was dominated by cowboys and never seriously pursued the cowgirls' special interests.

While cowgirl athletes were being forced out of rodeo, a new group of cowgirl look-alikes were welcomed with open arms. They were the "sponsor girls," young women who were nominated by their local communities to compete in beauty contests. As ranch-country debutantes, their job was to "add a little charm and glamor" to the testosterone-soaked world of male athleticism. Although the girls had to prove they could stay on a horse, the prizes were actually awarded on the basis of costume and looks, as those attributes were assessed by a panel of male judges. In most cases, a competent working cowgirl who could rope and ride had little or no chance against a pretty young thing with a rich daddy, who could afford to deck herself out in fancy cowgirl clothes. Soon, "ranch glamor girls" and queen contests were standard features of rodeos across the continent.

Cowgirls had always claimed territory on both sides of the gender divide. They had asked to be valued for both their "manly" skills and their "womanly" charms. They were energetic, masterful and modern—ambition personified—a perfect icon for the American spirit before

A Rodeo of Their Own

By the mid-forties, cowgirls could no longer compete as athletes on the pro-rodeo circuit. Although a few women continued to find work as contract performers, most were limited to sponsor contests or to serving as glamor girls in parades and production numbers.

The up-and-coming generation of working cowgirls hated these restrictions. They wanted to be judged on their skills rather than their appearance. If their riding abilities were to be assessed by racing around barrels, then the course should not be altered halfway through the contest. Races should be timed to the split second, with no extra points for the girl who looked best in tight pants. When cowgirls threatened to boycott local rodeos unless these rules were enforced, barrel racing began to develop as a legitimate event.

In 1948, a group of cowgirls came together to pursue these, and other, demands. As the first organization of female pro athletes in the United States, the Girls Rodeo Association was designed to promote the participation of women in all aspects of the sport. One of its priorities was to develop a circuit of All-Girl Rodeos in which women could compete in bronc riding, bull riding, steer roping and other rough-stock events. Another was to work for the readmission of women to the high-profile competitions such as the Madison Square Garden rodeo and, later, the National Finals Rodeo. A degree of success was finally achieved in 1967, when women's barrel racing was added to the NFR program. Equal prizes for the women's event were not attained until twelve years later, when the women again threatened to withdraw unless their demands were met.

Today, the Women's Professional Rodeo Association (the successor of the GRA) has over a thousand members, and barrel racing can claim its first million-dollar cowgirl in the person of Charmayne James Rodman. In Canada, the Canadian Girls Rodeo Association has been working on behalf of women's rodeo since 1957. Like the WPRA, it is and always has been run and managed by women.

Thena Mae Farr and Nancy Binford, top, helped to found the Girls Rodeo Association. Today, most of the association's members are involved in barrel racing, a women-only sport. Faye Blackstone, right, demonstrates the speed and skill that made her a state champion in the fifties. *National Cowgirl Hall of Fame and Western Heritage Center*

Calendar cowgirls of the forties and fifties ranged from

sweet and sunny to decidedly saucy. *Right, Courtesy of*

McQuarrie's Tea and Coffee Merchants, Saskatoon,

Saskatchewan

1929. But as the roar of the twenties faded away during the Depression, the public sought the solace of a cozier, less challenging vision. Even cowgirls were forced into their "rightful" place, on the feminine side of the line. By the mid-thirties, being a cowgirl had become just another way of making a fashion statement. For the first time, department stores stocked women's Levi's and western boots, and outdoorsy cowgirl styles were celebrated in the pages of *Vogue*. Fashion writers for *Life* magazine, circa 1940, commented approvingly on "the dude girls of the West," who were "taking to nifty riding clothes with fancy skirts and pants." The main concern of the new cowgirl was always to look her best.

As cowgirl style was shifted away from its roots, it became available to anyone who wished to appropriate it. A housewife or a secretary could buy it off the rack, and an advertiser could pick it up as a ready-made image. As visual *prêt-à-porter,* the cowgirl could be made to stand for different things in different contexts. As seen through the ad man's distorting lens, she could be the healthy horseback rider who smoked cigarettes, the free spirit who drove fast cars or the perky sexpot who ate Pangburn chocolates. She could be the fresh-faced, innocent country child that was used to promote the down-home values of local businesses. Rarely, if ever, was she shown as a strong, competent person who could hold her own in a man's world. The cowgirl was in the process of becoming just another female "look" that could be used to draw attention to consumer goods.

As image piled upon image, the cowgirl's meaning was blurred, but her original feisty spirit was not totally obscured. One of the women who kept it alive during the 1930s was a country singer who rose to fame as Patsy Montana. Born Ruby Blevins in Arkansas in 1912, Patsy came to her western identity first as "the yodelling cowgirl from San Antone," and a little later as a member of a trio called the Montana Cowgirls. By the time she was 21, she had signed on as female vocalist with a hot country string band (the Prairie Ramblers) and was well on her way to becoming a star of the National Barn Dance, a hugely successful country and western radio program that was broadcast across the United States. A couple of years later, in 1935, she crowned this success with a million-selling hit record, the first ever credited to a female country artist.

This well-dressed young cowhand with her braided quirt was photographed in the foothills of Alberta in 1951. *Provincial Archives of Alberta PA1899/1*

97

FACING PAGE. The cowgirl "look" was first popularized in the thirties by a vogue for dude-ranch holidays. These beautifully turned-out "dudines" were guests at the Valley Ranch in 1935. *Buffalo Bill Historical Center, Cody, Wyoming, Irving H. "Larry" Larom Collection* THIS PAGE, TOP. In the forties and fifties, the cowgirl image could be used to sell almost anything, from cigarettes to sweet potatoes. The Old Gold cowgirl of 1952 invited smokers into a world of simple pleasures, without any of the exaggerated health claims that were then being made for other brands of cigarettes. RIGHT. In the summer of 1947, *McCall's Needlework Magazine* recommended western-style shirts as an "active sports vogue" for "playtime." *McCall's Needlework, original copyright 1947, reprinted copyright 1996.*

Patsy topped the charts with a spirited little number called "I Want to Be a Cowboy's Sweetheart," one of the many songs that she wrote for herself. ("I had to write my own material," she says. "Nobody else was going to do it for me.") At a time when radio was often called "the housewife's companion," Patsy's strong, sunny voice expressed a woman's straightforward desire for fresh air and freedom, cowgirl-style. She sang of galloping into the wind, sleeping near the cattle and yodelling at the top of her lungs, far from the constraints of the city. Her cowboy companion scarcely came into the picture, as she enjoyed the romance of her own high spirits and independence.

Fifty years later, Patsy was still amazed by the song's record-setting appeal. "It's a *girl's* number, and that ain't supposed to happen," she marvelled. But happen it did and, although her sales never broke through the heights again, Patsy continued to charm audiences with (among other things) her cheerful, danceable tributes to female exuberance. Married in 1934 and a mother by the next year, she went right on singing about cowgirls who refused to "settle down and be a wife." In a song called "The She-Buckaroo"(1936), she gives voice to a "tough-ridin'" rodeo cowgirl and "a man-hatin' lassie." In a similar vein, her "Rip Snortin' Two-Gun Gal" of 1939 makes the most of being "tough as I can be." And a 1941 session with the Sons of the Pioneers still finds her good-humoredly insisting that "Gals can do what cowhands do, deep in the Heart of Texas."

"At the time, I was just trying to make a living," Montana admits. "I never knew I was doing anything important for women until people started writing about me." While it's hard to say what her spunky lyrics meant to her female fans, her effect on the women of country music is easier to document. Before Patsy Montana made her breakthrough, female musicians had been forced into the role of the shy, sweet country gal. But by cheerfully asserting the cowgirl's right to yodel alongside the men, Patsy established a performance style that served country singers from Louise Massey and the Girls of the Golden West in the thirties and forties to the young Patsy Cline and on to k. d. lang and Emmylou Harris.

In addition to her other accomplishments, Patsy Montana wrote more than two hundred songs. She has been honored by the National Cowgirl Hall of Fame and the Academy of Country Music, among others. *Country Music Foundation*

FACING PAGE. In 1938, Jeanette MacDonald starred in a charming musical version of David Belasco's much-adapted story *The Girl of the Golden West*, with Buddy Ebsen as the flute-playing Alabama and Nelson Eddy as the dashing bandit Ramirez. *Photofest (Turner Entertainment)*

Sisters Dolly and Millie Good (or Goad) became well known in the thirties as "The Girls of the Golden West." Their repertoire included "My Love Is a Rider," a song commonly attributed to Belle Starr. *Courtesy of Liz Masterson*

FACING PAGE. In just four years, from 1940 to 1943, pretty, spunky Nell O'Day played the female lead in eighteen B-westerns. *Empire Publishing*

If women were beginning to make their way in western music, the same could not be said for western movies. Patsy Montana appeared in just one film, a 1939 potboiler for cowboy singer Gene Autry called *Colorado Sunset*. Her role, like that of the other women in the cast, was unimportant. As one critic has observed, "the Gene Autry era produced the heroine it deserved, a rigorously permanent-waved cowgirl in fringes and boots," whose main duty was to smile approvingly whenever the hero opened his golden throat. One welcome exception was a suite of movies, all from the late thirties, that featured a smooth-voiced singer named Dorothy Page. In *Singing Cowgirl*, *Ride 'Em Cowgirl* and *Water Rustlers*, Page stars as Shirley Martin, a ranch girl who capably foils the bad guys despite her womanly aversion to violence. In *Water Rustlers*, for example, she rallies the community to her side with an eloquent speech, masterminds the destruction of a dam that threatens local ranches, rescues the hero by lassoing him from a raging flood, and still finds time to croon a tune about life in the saddle.

Handicapped as they were by stingy budgets, Dorothy Page's films were not box-office hits. But the same misfortune did not befall the one major cowgirl film of the thirties—RKO Radio Pictures' 1935 biopic *Annie Oakley*. The star of the show was an up-and-comer from Brooklyn named Barbara Stanwyck (née Ruby Stevens), who was making her first western picture. A self-made star with a perfect understanding of Oakley's working-class drive, Stanwyck had been supporting herself since her early teens, when she got work, first, in the sixteenth row of the Ziegfeld Follies, and a little later, as a chorus girl in Miss Guinan's speakeasies. Although Stanwyck had grown up on westerns rather than in the West, she shared her employer's enthusiasm for cowgirl heroines. In later years, she would repeatedly complain about the standard western plot in which the women were left behind "with the kids and the cows" while the men went boldly forth to defend their interests.

"Nuts to the kids and the cows," Stanwyck snorted. And nuts to the producers who thought frontier women had done nothing except keep house. You had only to read your history to know ranch wives had done more. "They were in cattle drives. They were *there*." And while they weren't exactly feminine, with their breeches and guns, "don't kid yourself," she admonished, "they were female!" Western women had stood as equals with their men, and Stanwyck wanted a chance to do justice to them.

PLAYING "THE GIRL"

I was referred to as "the girl." The girl had to hit her marks, which were chalk marks on the floor or the dirt, in order to receive the best light. [Cameraman] Ted [McCord] took the effort to give me the best light he could . . . The girl had to play her scenes right because there were no second takes and, horrors, of course no retakes. The main stars were coached but not the girls.

—Ruth Hall, about her role
in *Dynamite Ranch*, 1932

On the first day of the picture, I was supposed to get on a horse. I went over to [actor] Bob Livingstone and whispered, "Which side of the horse am I supposed to get up on?" I knew enough to know there was a right and wrong side but not which was which. Bob helped me and didn't snitch on me. I've always been grateful about that. In those days, you'd get a lead in a B-western and that'd be your training. They'd pay you a hundred dollars and it would take about a week to do it.

—Myrna Dell, about her work in
Raiders of Red Gap, early 1940s

In *Annie Oakley*, she took on this challenge at one remove, as she portrayed a woman who had herself portrayed a western girl. But even so Stanwyck ran head on into the woman-tamers. The scriptwriters granted Miss Oakley her skill as a sharpshooter and even permitted her lover to admire her competence. ("I know you can beat me [at shooting], and I'm proud of you," he says. "I never thought I'd see the day I could stand that.") But what the filmmakers could not stand was Oakley's on-target purposefulness. The real Annie Oakley had been a professional who, with her husband's support, had focused all her energy on her shooting career. The movie Annie, by contrast, is a fool for love who would willingly give up all she's achieved for the sake of her man.

Thus, unlike the historic Annie who bested Frank Butler with glee, Stanwyck's Annie lets her lover save face by winning. As sad music wells behind her, her mother leans over to warn that she wouldn't want to be the cause of the young man losing his job. But Annie has her own reason for throwing the match. "I couldn't beat that fellow," she says. "He was just too pretty." As the film ends, she dashes out of the Wild West ring and into her lover's arms, apparently with the intention of leaving show business behind. For, as Sitting Bull has reminded her, "papooses good" for a woman.

The hand that rocks the cradle has to drop the gun. Even the determined Miss Oakley has a woman's heart, and her steel-eyed resolve melts away in the sweet sunshine of love. As Hollywood never tired of asserting (to generous applause), this is what real women want.

But this certitude was briefly challenged by the outbreak of World War II and an urgent need for women to join the labor force. "The more women are at war, the sooner we'll win" ran a U.S. government slogan. Now was the moment for a stalwart heroine who could back up Our Brave Boys with her devotion, courage and stoic self-sacrifice—someone exactly like the matriarch Hannah McCrea, whom Stanwyck played in a wartime western called *The Great Man's Lady* (1942). A pioneering cattle woman who survived more than her share of trials, Hannah devoted her entire long life to serving her husband's aims. As comely as she was iron-willed, she was the perfect backup for a man with heroic goals. So, too, was the six-gun-toting cowgirl, played by Ella Raines, who won the hand and heart of John Wayne in *Tall in the Saddle* (1944). "Meaner 'n a skilletful of rattlesnakes," and sexy besides, she was the woman you wanted to have by your side as you faced the bad guys.

When the war was over, women were sent back home, and softer domestic virtues came back into vogue. As Bette Davis explained it in 1950 in *All About Eve*, "being a woman" was the one career that no female could escape. "Sooner or later, we've got to work at it, no matter what other careers we've had or wanted. And in the last analysis nothing is any good unless you can look up just before dinner—or turn in bed—and there he is. Without that you're not a woman. You're someone with a French provincial office—or a book of clippings. But you're not a woman."

This anxious reiteration of what a woman is, and is not, would buzz through the cowgirl movies of the postwar period. And surprisingly, suddenly, there was a spate of them. Not only was Barbara Stanwyck back, in films like *The Furies* (1950), *Cattle Queen of Montana* (with Ronald Reagan, 1954)

and *Forty Guns* (1957), but other big names were also cast in cowgirl roles. In three successive years in the early fifties, Jane Russell ran with the Dalton gang in *Montana Belle* (1952); Doris Day kicked up her heels as *Calamity Jane* (1953); and Joan Crawford and Mercedes McCambridge shot it out with each other in *Johnny Guitar* (1954). In the same era, B-movie bad girl Marie Windsor starred as the outlaw Doll Brown in *Hellfire* (1949), Barbara Britton played a masked avenger in *Bandit Queen* (1950), sheriff Beverly Garland avenged her husband's death in *Gunslinger* (1956)—and there were many others.

At a time when cowboy movies were losing viewers to TV, the introduction of female heroes was an attempt to bring new life to a genre that had always maintained itself through "endless repetition with a difference." But the simple substitution of a woman for a man turned out to be not at all simple in its consequences. In fact, it entirely changed the focus of the action. Instead of the familiar themes of cowboy adventures—nature vs. culture, violence vs. the law—any

Ethel Merman was improbably cast as Annie Oakley in the 1946 stage version of Rogers and Hammerstein's hit musical *Annie Get Your Gun*. In this retelling of her story, Miss Oakley throws the shooting match with Frank Butler (which the historical Annie won) but is reconciled to her loss because "You Can't Get a Man with a Gun." *Photofest*

FACING PAGE. The presence of Barbara Stanwyck as the straight-shooting heroine more than compensates for the inaccuracies in RKO Radio Picture's 1935 film biography of Annie Oakley. *Photofest (Turner Entertainment)*

By the early forties, the cowgirl image had become associated with a range of sometimes contradictory meanings. A cowgirl might be a strong, effective woman who was respected and loved by strong men, like the heroines of *Ranch Romances*' short fiction. Or she might be a bimbo, like the *Saturday Evening Post*'s covergirl, who seems vapidly unaware of the cowboys' leering appraisal. *Below, The Curtis Publishing Company*

Love Stories of the Real West

RANCH ROMANCES

15c

ERIC HOWARD

Snarling Gold
By CLEE WOODS

Second April Number

THE SATURDAY EVENING POST

JUNE 20, 1942

BIBLE OF BASEBALL
And the Story of its Creator, the Game's Greate Unsung Hero

FACING PAGE. In 1943, a gun-toting Dorothy Dandridge appeared in a "soundie," or musical short, for a tune called "Moo Cow Boogie." *American Museum of the Moving Image, Courtesy of the Ernie Smith Collection*

western that starred a female immediately became transfixed by her gender. Could a woman be tough and attractive? Could she be sexual without being bad? What happened when she followed her own star instead of submitting to men? Could she fight back against male bullies and sexual abuse? Could a woman stick to her guns, even if it led to her death?

This was the fifties, remember, and a decade before Betty Friedan set a match to middle-class women's anger. Out in suburbia, women were doing their best to be (in the words of Irving Berlin's 1946 musical "tribute" to Annie Oakley) "as soft and as pink as a nursery." And yet questions about gender were being explored in—of all places—cowgirl westerns!

It's not that these movies were "feminist" in their intentions or in their plots. Indeed, the scriptwriters took some pains to rein in their high-riding stars. Maria Hart, the determined heroine of *Cattle Queen* (1951), is ultimately forced to submit to her lover's authority. ("So far you've had everything your way," he says in the closing scenes. "From now on it's going to be mine.") And a 1957 western called *The Dalton Girls* had the unusual luxury of taming four women at once, when its family of female outlaws is brought to justice. In the gun battle that brings the film to a close, two of the sisters are killed, one collapses in the arms of her suitor, and the leader is dragged off bawling for someone to take her home.

But the primary pleasure of western films is not in their denouements; it is in the action that leads up to them. It's fun to watch the Cattle Queen beat the boys to the pass and even more fun when she's given a chance to gloat about it. "To beat a man at his own game," she crows, "a woman not only has to be as good. She's got to be better." It's satisfying to see a woman stand up to a rapist, as Holly Dalton does, and to cheer for her and her sisters when they pull off their daring holdups. ("I have a great respect for ladies," one of their victims quips. "Especially those with revolvers.") When Barbara Stanwyck, as Kit Banyan in *The Maverick Queen* (1956), heads a bad guy off a cliff and rolls a log down after him, we admire both her muscle and her quick thinking. The outlaw boss Butch Cassidy speaks for us when he says, "That's what I like about you, Kit. You can always take care of yourself."

Barbara Stanwyck steels herself for a fight in *Cattle Queen of Montana*, 1954. The Blackfoot Indians who worked on this picture honored Stanwyck with the title of Princess Many Victories III, because of her courage as a stuntwoman. *Photofest*

FACING PAGE. Joan Crawford was the headliner in *Johnny Guitar*, a perverse and nervy psychological western. *Photofest (Republic)*

Few movie cowgirls were allowed to be tough through and through. Jane Russell, left, traded in her mannish outlaw gear to perform as a dancehall girl in *Montana Belle* (1952); cheesecake cowgirls displayed their charms in *Two Guys From Texas* (1948), and Joan Leslie was caricatured in an outrageously eroticized poster for *Woman They Almost Lynched* (1953), a film that, despite its salacious advertising, was not a skin flick. *Photofest (RKO Pictures)/(Turner Entertainment)/(Republic)*

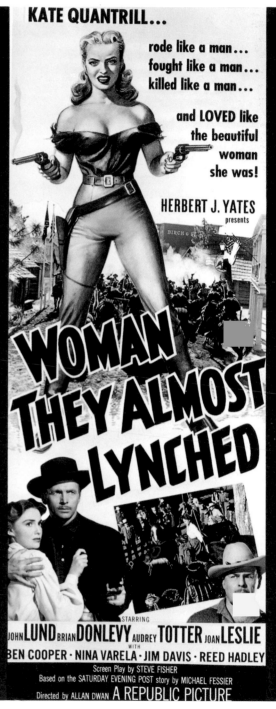

More Cowgirl Flicks

Cat Ballou (1965) is a delightful western comedy in which Jane Fonda comes home to the ranch to find her father threatened by developers. With an improbable crew of helpers, she sets out to avenge his death.

The Ballad of Josie (1968) casts Doris Day as a turn-of-the-century suffragist in Wyoming who defends herself against her husband's violence and then sets out to support herself on her own sheep ranch.

Hannie Caulder (1971) is a shoot-'em-up with Raquel Welch in the title role. A revenge story, it follows Hannie as she pursues and kills the three men who raped her and murdered her husband. Ms. Welch in a poncho is highly decorative.

Comes a Horseman (1978) presents Jane Fonda and James Caan as ranchers who are threatened by cattle barons. Considered by most critics to be "a major western."

Heartland (1979) is a highly acclaimed evocation of the life of Wyoming homesteader Elinore Pruitt Stewart, as she described it in her letters.

Even Cowgirls Get the Blues (1994) is a less-than-successful film adaptation of Tom Robbins's quirky novel about lesbian cowgirls on the Rubber Rose Ranch, with Uma Thurman, Rain Phoenix and Lorraine Bracco.

The Quick and the Dead (1995) features Sharon Stone as a gunfighter in a campy movie about the ritual gun duel. Forgettable.

There was also another way—less obvious and even less intentional—in which fifties' cowgirl movies promoted the cause of female independence. Many of these movies are truly bad, so bad that there is little sustained development of the central character. Instead she is shown in a series of vignettes, each no doubt meant to portray a different aspect of her complex and fascinating female nature. In one scene she is riding hell-for-leather across the prairie landscape; in the next, she is in her gingham dress hanging out the wash; in yet another, she is slinking around in a lacy grown making eyes at men. With every change of clothes comes a change of manner and voice, and an unannounced change in the meaning of womanliness. Being a woman, it seems, might be just a series of roles, each of which could be put on and off with a change of clothes.

This subtle point may have escaped mere adults, but it was certainly not lost on the children who grew up with westerns. As little girls in the fifties, we knew that wearing our Sunday best meant we were expected to "act" like little ladies. As we were constantly reminded, ladies were quiet, kept their clothes clean and sat with their knees together. But the second we put on a cowboy hat or strapped on a holster and guns, a whole new range of options was suddenly open to us. Now we could shout and shoot and tear around with the boys; we had legs for chasing, lungs for yelling and energy to burn. Our mentor in this transformation was not a film actress, but the woman who brought the cowgirl into our homes each week on television. Her name, of course, was Dale Evans.

The Law Lady

In an episode of The Lone Ranger *that was broadcast on TV in 1954, the "masked rider" and Tonto come upon a poster signed by Mrs. Richard Lee, Sheriff.*

Tonto: Woman sheriff, Kemo sabe? We never hear of that before.

Lone Ranger: Some time ago, the Wyoming legislature passed a law giving the women right here to vote and hold office.

Tonto: Uh, that may be good idea.

L.R.: It is good, Tonto. Some day every woman in the United States will have the same right.

Tonto: You think her elected to office after husband killed?

L.R.: Perhaps, but the governor may have appointed her to fill out her husband's unexpired term.

Tonto: Uh, that be hard job for woman.

Before the Lone Ranger and Tonto can go to the aid of the lady sheriff, they are arrested by a male deputy, who mistakes them for outlaws.

L.R.: I take it then Mrs. Lee hasn't had much success in dealing with the outlaws in this territory.

Deputy: Success? Humpf. A woman sheriff?

Tonto: You not like idea of woman in that job?

Deputy: Nobody in Gunstock likes the idea . . . A sheriff's office is no place for frills and ribbons. A woman belongs in her own home with her own man and her own children—especially a woman as pretty as—

L.R.: As pretty as Mrs. Lee?

Deputy: We've wasted enough time.

With the help of the Lone Ranger, Mrs. Lee captures the bad guys and brings them to justice.

Deputy: I guess I made my share of mistakes. And the biggest one was being so stubborn about a woman holding office. I hear the people in town are mighty proud of their sheriff. They want you to run again, Clare, and I do too.

Clare Lee: But I don't. Being a sheriff is a man's job. [She gives her badge to the deputy.] However, I may run for the county board of commissioners.

Deputy: Then I insist at least on being your campaign manager.

Linda Stirling played Zorro's sister in a 1944 serial called *Zorro's Black Whip*. Empire Publishing FACING PAGE. B-western stalwart Ruth Roman appeared in *Belle Starr's Daughter* in 1948. *Photofest* OVERLEAF. In *Hellfire* (1949), Marie Windsor presented the outlaw Doll Brown in her many guises, from lady to dancehall gal to housewife to bandit. Womanliness, it seemed, might be little more than a clever performance. *Photofest*

Frances Octavia Smith was born in Ulvade, Texas, in 1912 and grew up there and in small-town Arkansas. A precocious, headstrong child, she married at fourteen and was deserted a year later. A single mother with a young child to support (and determined to go it alone), she worked in an office by day and sang on the radio at night. "My greatest goal was to make a name for myself in show business," she recalls, but the economy was grim, and at times she almost starved. Finally, in 1939—by now as Dale Evans—she found work as the lead vocalist with an orchestra and soon thereafter was called to Hollywood. Her dream was to star as a glamor-girl singer in musicals. Instead, in 1944, she was cast opposite Roy Rogers in *The Cowboy and the Senorita*.

The invitation to play this role was, as she later put it, not "the most exciting proposal I'd ever heard." But "before the year was out I had three more pictures with Roy and, when fan mail began arriving in amounts far greater than at any time in my career, it occurred to me that riding horses, holding the reins, and saying 'He went thataway' wasn't the worst fate that could befall a girl." By 1947, she had settled so comfortably into her new role that she married her leading man. That same year, she became the first and only woman to make the annual listing of the Top Ten western movie stars, an achievement she would repeat several times in the early 1950s. Dale Evans, the reluctant cowgirl, had earned the right to bill herself as "Queen of the West."

As Roy Rogers saw it, Dale went over so well with the fans because she refused to stand around smiling and looking cute. "When Dale came along, she got into the fights and everything!" he enthused. "She gave the leading lady a better part, and the people liked it!" So when the couple launched themselves on children's TV in 1951, Dale was cast as an independent businesswoman, the owner of the Eureka Café in Mission City. As in their movies, there was to be no real romance, just (as Roy described it) "friendship and a combining of efforts to solve the problems and right the wrongs the scriptwriters came up with." In fact, Dale's piece of the action was always much smaller than Roy's—and even than Trigger's, at times—and she spent much of her time making coffee, serving sandwiches and mothering anyone who seemed to need it. Still, she could always be counted on when the going got rough. Being a womanly woman, she kept out of the

Dale saved the day in the October–December edition of *Dale Evans, Queen of the West*, 1956. *Courtesy of the Roy Rogers and Dale Evans Museum, Victorville, California*

116

DELL

OCT.-DEC.

10¢

Queen of the West
DALE EVANS

fisticuffs, but otherwise she was capable and fearless. She'd gallop away on Buttermilk with an urgent message for Roy or hold a villain at gun point until he could be dealt with by the boys. If the bad guys managed to capture her, she could sometimes get herself out of harm. As sidekick Pat Brady once put it, Miss Evans was "pretty smart."

Miss Evans was even smarter when she got away from Roy. In her comics and Viewmaster stories, she was clearly the star. She could retrieve her gun from a team of crooks with a quick flick of her whip or capture three armed hoodlums without so much as breaking into a sweat. Although her detective work often had a feminine touch, as she deciphered clues written in lipstick or baked into cakes, she was smart, unafraid and independent. (When she set out to investigate a crime in one comic-book story, her sidekick offered to keep her company, but she turned him down. "I can look around better alone," she insisted.) By the final frame, she inevitably had the bad guys locked up. "Everything's all right," someone would say. "Thanks to Dale!!"

While Dale Evans was setting things straight around Mission City, another TV cowgirl was hard at work in the town of Diablo, somewhere in the southwest corner of the Indian Territory. Beginning in 1953, Diablo was the TV home town of none other than Annie Oakley, as played—in perpetual pigtails—by Gail Davis. Like her famous namesake, this young Annie was a crack shot, but she was also a cook, a caregiver (to her small brother, Tagg), a daring trickrider, a roper, a teamster and a tracking expert. There was nothing she couldn't do well. Even the sheriff, her Uncle Luke, took advice and direction from her. "You've got a head on your shoulders, Annie," he once said. Other men sometimes talked down to her and tried to keep her at home, but Annie never allowed herself to be sidelined for long. She had to stop the runaway stage and save Tagg from rattlesnake bites. Most of all, she had to outsmart the criminals and save her neighbors from harm.

It was all good fun, of course—just a half-hour's entertainment for the tykes. But for some of us "little ladies," sprawled in front of the box or turning the pages of the latest comic book, Annie and Dale were more than a simple diversion. These cowgirls were our idols and they beckoned us into their world—a world of fantasy in which girls and women could (however provisionally) be heroes. When we strapped on toy six-shooters, we were ready to take on the world. If our parents wouldn't let us have guns of our own, we borrowed them from the boys. If our playmates thought we should run the café, we refused to play by their rules. True to the cowgirl spirit, we wanted into the game as equals.

Far too soon, our cowgirl heroines left us to struggle on alone. After hitting "the bull's eye of entertainment" for eighty-one episodes, *Annie Oakley* went out of production in 1956. *The*

"Yuh're as Good as Two Men!"

In general, comic books don't have much use for capable females. There's Wonder Woman, to be sure, but has there been anyone else? Well, how about K-Bar-Kate, Rhoda Trail and Buckskin Belle? These are just three of the cowgirl heroes who flourished briefly in the western comics of the postwar period.

At the same time as women were roughing it up in western films, these characters kept readers turning the pages of comic books like *Bill West, The Hawk* and *Western Crime-Busters. Blazing West,* for example, featured a voluptuous deputy sheriff named Buffalo Belle Trent, "the red head who caught 'em red-handed in the days of the Cherokee Strip!" Belle is a looker, with her big bust and short skirts, but she is no one to be trifled with. "I'm a gal who riles fast," she warns the bad guys in one story—"an' it starts with muh trigger finger!" When a sleazy crook in another issue tries to steal a kiss, she flattens him with her fist. "I can play the sweet innocent role just so long," she explains, "but I draw the line at maulin'!"

To the hombres that run afoul of her, Buffalo Belle is a "gun totin' cyclone," "a murderin' she-coyote," and a plain old "ornery female." Prairie Kate is called a "danged skirt," and Rhoda Trail's a "little tomcat." But this abuse is all forgotten when, against the most terrible odds, the heroine of the story brings the bad guys in. Then she may hear the ultimate praise: "Doggone, yuh're as good as two men." The world of comic books has not seen her like again.

The lead-slinging Buckskin Belle appeared in the March 1955 edition of *The Hawk*. Rhoda Trail an' her Gramps, as drawn by Anthony Cataldo, were featured in *Bill West* for February 1951. *Courtesy of Jack Shadoian*

Roy Rogers Show followed suit a year later (though Roy and Dale lived on in reruns until the mid-sixties and even later through their recordings and personal appearances). By 1965, about the only small-screen cowgirl left was the indefatigable Barbara Stanwyck, who flourished as ranch owner Victoria Barkley on ABC's *The Big Valley*. "I'm a tough old broad," she informed the producers when they approached her about the show. "If you want someone to tiptoe down the Barkley staircase in crinoline and politely ask where the cattle went, get another girl." But they wanted her, and they wrote her the part she deserved. As Stanwyck described her, Victoria Barkley was an "old broad" like herself, who conducted herself with a mixture of guts and elegance. The first cowgirl to star in an adult TV western, she was also the last.

When *The Big Valley* went off the air in 1969, an era came to a close. The day of the heroic cowgirl was over, and a bevy of country cuties now reigned in her stead. Direct descendants of the "ranch glamor girls" who had come on the scene in the thirties and forties, these new cowgirls looked more at home in beauty pageants or rodeo parades than on the backs of bucking broncs. They had style instead of substance, glitter instead of guts. Although the movies still sometimes featured women in cowgirl roles—Raquel Welch in *Hannie Caulder* (1971), Sharon Stone in *The Quick and the Dead* (1995)—the concept no longer made sense. Barbie dolls in Stetsons could not pass as western heroines.

Like many a "shrew" before and since, the cowgirl had been tamed. From the beginning, her critics had been eager to bring her down a peg. In time, they succeeded in transforming her into less than she really was—just a sexy little country gal in fancy western duds. Today, people sometimes point to this figure as a reminder of days gone by, when Men Were Men and women existed only to please them. But history says otherwise. The cowgirl represents a tradition of women's ambition and strength, a heritage that can be traced back for more than a century. From Lizzie Williams to Barbara Stanwyck, she embodied a working girl's pride; and from the Old West to the western, she had fought to keep that spirit alive. If the cowgirl was bucked off in the end—my God, did she have a ride!

"You can't trust a man
Cause a man will lie
But a gun stays beside you
Till the day you die.
A man is a cheater
With his triflin' ways
But a gun's always faithful
Cause a gun never strays."
—"A GUN IS MY LIFE,"
song from THE DALTON GIRLS, *1957*

FACING PAGE. Gail Davis starred in the *Annie Oakley* TV series, perhaps the best programming for girls that has yet been produced. *Photofest*

The three Oliver sisters posed with their horses at the Diamond L Ranch, near Millarville, Alberta, in the 1930s. *Glenbow Archives, Calgary, Alberta, NB37-21*
FACING PAGE. Jonnie Jonckowski, one of the relatively small number of women to compete in roughstock rodeo events in the 1980s and 1990s, is a two-time world champion bull rider. "It didn't take guts for me to ride bulls," she says. "It took guts to buck the people who didn't want me to do it." *Courtesy of Jonnie Jonckowski*

Meanwhile, Back at the Ranch

The first generation of ranch women and girls had worked alongside the men and had often shared in the ownership of herds and land. But as times became more settled and "civilization" moved west, bourgeois values reasserted themselves. Wealth passed into male control and, as much as possible, women were herded back into the kitchen.

Womanly nature being what it is, they were not all willing to go. What's more, many small outfits couldn't afford to do without their labor. When Gertrude Rogers Hall married into the Cruikshank Ranch in the Great Sand Hills of Saskatchewan in 1944, she found herself responsible for cleaning, cooking, baking, churning, washing, mending and childcare as well as for outside work during calving and branding seasons. At about the same time, Eulalia Bourne homesteaded on her own small place in Arizona and later worked as a "cowboy" for two successive husbands. When she eventually found herself "de-spoused," she made a success of the ranch on her own. Every ranch community has many stories like theirs.

Women also continued to work as paid hands. Up in Saskatchewan, Delores Noreen hired on with the Slade Ranch at Tompkins in the late thirties. "Nobody could get a job back then," she says. "I got a job." By the end of her long work life, she was the ranch's foreman and today, in her seventies, she still sometimes rides with its cattle. Cowgirl poet Georgie Sicking is another woman who started work as a cowhand in the thirties and made a career as a "cowboy" and rancher. In retrospect, she says, "I am truly thankful that I had the courage to stand by my own convictions and didn't give in to be just another housewife."

Today, most family ranches are husband-and-wife operations. The working cowgirl is still very much with us.

NOTES

The numbers on the left refer to page numbers. Notes refer to direct quotations only. For a complete listing of sources, please consult the references.

REAL COWBOY GIRLS

1. Mollie, as quoted by Sandra L. Myres, *Westering Women and the Frontier Experience 1800–1915*, p. 236.

3. "No cowgirls" comments by Edward Brado, *Cattle Kingdom: Early Ranching in Alberta*, p. 19; Larry Goodwyn, "The Frontier Myth and Southwestern Literature," quoted by Evelyn King, *Women on the Cattle Trail and in the Roundup*, p. 3; Larry McMurtry, *In a Narrow Grave*, quoted by Elizabeth Maret, *Women of the Range: Women's Role in the Texas Beef Cattle Industry*, p. xiii; Patrick A. Dunae, ed., *Ranchers' Legacy: Alberta Essays by Lewis G. Thomas*, p. 16; Lizzie Williams described by Ann Fears Crawford and Crystal Sasse Ragsdale, *Women in Texas: Their Lives, Their Experiences, Their Accomplishments*, p. 120.

4. Anthony Trollope, as quoted by Myres, *Westering Women and the Frontier Experience*, p. 261; Lizzie Williams described by Crawford and Ragsdale, *Women in Texas*, p. 121.

5. Ann Burke story as quoted by Maret, *Women of the Range*, p. 34; ranch wife Mary Kate Cruze, "A Pioneer Mother's Experience," in *The Trail Drivers of Texas*, edited by J. Marvin Hunter (New York: Argosy-Antiquarian, 1963; 874–81), p. 879; Belle Barton, as described in "Their Honeymoon Trail in 1874," p. 14.

7. The brands are reproduced from Jack Jackson, *Los Mesteños: Spanish Ranching in Texas*, pp. 646–48; Mrs. A. Burks, "A Woman Trail Driver," p. 305.

8. Samuel Dunn Houston, "When a Girl Masqueraded as a Cowboy and Spent Four Months on the Trail," in *The Trail Drivers of Texas*, edited by J. Marvin Hunter (New York: Argosy-Antiquarian, 1963; 71–78), pp. 75–77;

jilted cowgirl as quoted by Clifford P. Westermeier, *Trailing the Cowboy: His Life and Lore As Told by Frontier Journalists*, p. 324.

9. Mrs. E. J. Guerin, *Mountain Charley or the Adventures of Mrs. E. J. Guerin Who Was Thirteen Years in Male Attire*, pp. 19, 22; Fanny Seabride, as described in "A Daring Western Woman."

13. Middy Morgan story from *The North British Agriculturalist*, 30 June 1880, as quoted by Jordan, *Cowgirls*, p. 137.

15. Martha Ann Morrison, as quoted by Lillian Schlissel, *Women's Diaries of the Westward Journey*, p. 35; Miriam Davis, as quoted by Lillian Schlissel, "Frontier Families: Crisis in Ideology," p. 157; Theodore Roosevelt, as quoted by Billie Barnes Jensen, "'In the Weird and Wooly West': Anti-Suffrage Women, Gender Issues and Woman Suffrage in the West," p. 50; California lawmaker, as quoted by Mari J. Matsuda, "The West and the Legal Status of Women: Explanations of Frontier Feminism," p. 50; Abby Mansur, letter to her sister, 1852–54, reprinted in Christiane Fischer, ed., *Let Them Speak for Themselves: Women in the American West 1849–1900*, p. 51; Emerson Hough, as quoted by Brown, *The Gentle Tamers*, p. 11.

17. Elizabeth J. Thorpe on "appalling equality," as quoted by Paula M. Bauman, "Single Women Homesteaders in Wyoming, 1880–1930," p. 42; Mrs. A. N. Holm re old maids, as quoted by Susan A. Hallgarth, "Women Settlers on the Frontier: Unwed, Unreluctant, Unrepentant," p. 27; Elinore Pruitt Stewart, *Letters of a Woman Homesteader*, p. 134; other quotations about homesteading from Hallgarth, "Women Settlers on the Frontier," pp. 25, 26.

19. Unidentified woman, as quoted by Ruth Ann Alexander, "South Dakota Women Writers and the Blooming of the Pioneer Heroine, 1922–39," p. 305; Caroline Lockhart, 1918, as quoted by Necah Stewart Furman, *Caroline Lockhart: Her Life and Legacy*, back cover.

20. Catherine Neil, "Recollections of a Sheep Herder's Bride," *Alberta History* 35, no. 3, p. 22 and 36, no. 1, p. 19; Monica Hopkins, *Letters from a Lady Rancher*, pp. 89–90.

21. Evelyn Cameron, "A Woman's Big Game Hunting," as quoted by Donna M. Lucey, *Photographing Montana 1894–1928: The Life and Work of Evelyn Cameron*, p. 58; Stewart, *Letters of a Woman Homesteader*, p. 282.

22. Hopkins, *Letters from a Lady Rancher*, p. 127.

25. Agnes Morley Cleaveland, *No Life for a Lady*, pp. 37, 103, 127, 96, 129–30.

29. Cleaveland, *No Life for a Lady*, pp. 129–30; Ann Bassett Willis, "'Queen Ann' of Brown's Park," pp. 94–95; Joyce Gibson Roach, *The Cowgirls*, p. xxi.

30. Vivian Thorp McClarey, as quoted by Jordan, *Cowgirls*, p. 164.

32. *New York Times*, as quoted by Valerie Steele, *Fashion and Eroticism: Ideals of Feminine Beauty from the Victorian Era to the Jazz Age*, p. 146; Evelyn J. Cameron, "The 'Cowgirl' in Montana," pp. 830, 832; Willis, "'Queen Ann' of Brown's Park," p. 95.

33. Cleaveland, *No Life for a Lady*, p. 242.

34. Cameron, "The 'Cowgirl' in Montana," pp. 830, 832; Marie Bell and another ranch girl (Amy Chubb), as quoted by Teresa Jordan, *Cowgirls: Women of the American West*, pp. 25, 12; Willis, "'Queen Ann' of Brown's Park," pp. 93–94; Miriam Davis Colt, *Went to Kansas*, as quoted by Helvenston, "Ornament or Instrument?," p. 45.

36. Cattle Kate, as described in "A Double Lynching," *Cheyenne Daily Leader*, 23 July 1889, quoted by George W. Hufsmith, *The Wyoming Lynching of Cattle Kate, 1889*, p. 11; comment on ranch women from the *Union Sentinel* newspaper, 1864, as quoted by Sally I. Helvenston, "Ornament or Instrument? Proper Roles for Women on the Kansas Frontier," p. 36; plucky woman rancher, Cheyenne *Democratic Leader*, 1855, as quoted by Dee Brown, *The Gentle Tamers: Women of the Old Wild West*, p. 255.

37. "Our Little Cowgirl," as quoted by John A. Lomax, *Songs of the Cattle Trail and Cow Camp*, pp. 82–83.

FACING PAGE. The Misses McLeod and Robertson dressed up as frontierswomen in 1894. *Ernest Brown photo, B6741, Provincial Archives of Alberta*

39. Annie Oakley, as quoted by Glenda Riley, *The Life and Legacy of Annie Oakley*, p. 175.

41. Advertisement from *The Daily Record of the Times*, Willes-Barre, Pa., 27 November 1873, as reproduced in Joseph G. Rosa and Robin May, *Buffalo Bill and His Wild West: A Pictorial Biography*, p. 53.

42. Elizabeth Custer, as quoted by Don Russell, *The Lives and Legends of Buffalo Bill*, p. 323.

43. Buffalo Bill, as quoted by Rosa and May, *Buffalo Bill and His Wild West*, p. 81; Annie Oakley, as quoted by Isabelle S. Sayers, *Annie Oakley and Buffalo Bill's Wild West*, p. 4; Dexter Fellows and Andrew A. Freeman, *This Way to the Big Show*, as quoted by Sayers, *Annie Oakley and Buffalo Bill's Wild West*, p. 19.

45. Annie Oakley, as quoted by Riley, *The Life and Legacy of Annie Oakley*, pp. 133–34; Annie Oakley, as quoted by Riley, *The Life and Legacy of Annie Oakley*, p. 16.

47. Fellows and Freeman, as quoted by Sayers, *Annie Oakley and Buffalo Bill's Wild West*, p. 19; "Arizona" John Burke, as quoted by Glenda Riley, "Annie Oakley: Creating the Cowgirl," *Montana* version, p. 35; letter to the *Society Times*, 1887, as quoted by Riley, *The Life and Legacy of Annie Oakley*, p. 114; Queen Victoria, as quoted by Riley, *The Life and Legacy of Annie Oakley*, p. 41.

50. Womanly seclusion described in "A Lady's Gift," *Western Literary Journal and Monthly Review*, July 1836, as quoted by Myres, *Westering Women*, pp. 6–7; charm of femininity noted by F. C. Sumichrast, "Ladies at the Helm," *Outing* (1890), as quoted by Margery A. Bulger, "American Sportswomen in the 19th Century," p. 10; clean-limbed host described in "Montreal Sport," *Athletic Life*, 3 April 1896, p. 231, as quoted by Helen Lenskyj, "Physical Activity for Canadian Women, 1890–1930: Media Views," p. 212.

51. Women's Christian Temperance Union paper, as quoted by Banner, *American Beauty*, p. 140; Annie Oakley, as quoted by Riley, "Annie Oakley: Creating the Cowgirl," draft manuscript, p. 15.

52. Annie Oakley, as quoted by Riley, *The Life and Legacy of Annie Oakley*, p. 31.

54. Statement on women's rights by Buffalo Bill Cody, as quoted by Derry, "Corsets and Broncs," p. 12.

55. Annie Oakley, quoted by Damaine Vonada, "Annie Oakley Was More Than 'A Crack Shot in Petticoats,'" p. 144; James Fullarton Muirhead, *The Land of Contrasts: A Briton's View of His American Kin, 1898*, as quoted by Martha Banta, *Imaging American Women: Ideas and Ideals in Cultural History*, p. 96; Alexis de Tocqueville, 1838, as quoted by Lois W. Banner, *American Beauty*, p. 84; Hjamar Boyesen, "Types of American Women," 1908, as quoted by Banta, *Imaging American Women*, p. 99; Paul Bourget, *Outre-mer: notes sur l'Amérique*, p. 135; Henry James, *Daisy Miller*, 1879, as quoted by Banner, *American Beauty*, p. 84; May Lillie, as quoted by Glenn Shirley, *Pawnee Bill: A Biography of Major Gordon W. Lillie*, p. 187.

56. Letter re prejudice from Annie Oakley to "Mr. Conning Tower Man," 20 January 1917, Buffalo Bill Historical Center; praise for cowgirls from the *Illustrated London News*, 14 May 1887, as quoted by Rosa and May, *Buffalo Bill and His Wild West*, p. 116; advertisements quoted for Wild West shows by Kathryn Derry, "Corsets and Broncs: The Wild West Show Cowgirl, 1890–1920," p. 4.

59. Cleaveland, *No Life for a Lady*, p. 168.

60. Comment on Bertha Kapernick's ride, as quoted by Brown, *The Gentle Tamers*, pp. 42–43; race described in the *Cheyenne Leader*, 28 August 1901, as quoted by Mary L. Remley, "From Sidesaddle to Rodeo," p. 45.

61. Kapernick's ride described in the *Wyoming Tribune*, 31 August 1904, as quoted by Mary Lou LeCompte, *Cowgirls of the Rodeo: Pioneer Professional Athletes*, pp. 40–41.

62. Florence Weadick, as quoted by Donna Livingstone, unpublished biography of Guy Weadick, p. 32.

65. Guy Weadick, letter to Fanny Sperry, as quoted by LeCompte, *Cowgirls of the Rodeo*, p. 54; Tillie's ride described in *Winnipeg Tribune*, 13 August 1913, as quoted by LeCompte, *Cowgirls of the Rodeo*, p. 59.

66. Fanny Sperry, from Fanny Sperry Steele and Helen Clark, "A Horse Beneath Me . . . Sometimes," pp. 8–9, 12.

67. Alice Greenough, "What a Cowgirl Wants from Life," *Physical Culture*, May 1937, as quoted by Jordan, *Cowgirls*, pp. 222–23.

69. Leo Rodman, as quoted by Virginia Rowe Terrett, "(Mrs.) Ridin', Ropin', Wranglin' Rodman," p. 22.

73. Will Rogers, 1931, as quoted by Kathryn B. Stansbury, *Lucille Mulhall: Her Family, Her Life, Her Times*, p. 45; description of Fox Hastings as quoted by LeCompte, *Cowgirls of the Rodeo*, p. 90.

75. Bess Stephenson, "Cowgirl Cuties Just Girls A-Foot Backstage," *Fort Worth Star Telegram*, undated, quoted by Jordan, *Cowgirls*, p. 203.

76. Tad Lucas, as quoted by Jordan, *Cowgirls*, p. 203; Mabel DeLong Strickland, as quoted by Wills and Artho, *Cowgirl Legends*, p. 24.

79. Charles Simpson, *El Rodeo*, 1925, as quoted by Lajuana Newman, *Ruth Roach Salmon: A Pioneer Cowgirl*, p. 10.

80. Ollie Osborn, as quoted by LeCompte, *Cowgirls of the Rodeo*, p. 2; Alice Greenough, as quoted by Jordan, *Cowgirls*, p. 226; *New York Times*, 5 November 1922, as quoted by LeCompte, *Cowgirls of the Rodeo*, p. 82; Hutchins Hapgood, *Types from the City Streets*, 1910, as quoted by Banner, *American Beauty*, p. 199.

83. Vera McGinnis, as quoted by LeCompte, *Cowgirls of the Rodeo*, p. 31.

RHINESTONE COWGIRLS

85. The Dixie Chicks Cowgirl Band can be reached at 1450 Preston Forest Square, Ste. 212, Dallas, Texas 75230.

86. Texas Guinan, as quoted by Glenn Shirley, *"Hello Sucker!": The Story of Texas Guinan*, pp. 17–18.

89. Dell Dauntless, as quoted by Riley, *The Life and Legacy of Annie Oakley*, p. 174; rodeo cowgirl, re picnic as quoted by Roach, *The Cowgirls*, p. 171; Vera McGinnis, *Rodeo Road: My Life as a Pioneer Cowgirl*, p. 158.

90. Texas Guinan promos from Shirley, *"Hello Sucker!,"* pp. 38, 39; Texas Guinan on her movies, as quoted by Shirley, *"Hello Sucker!,"* p. 43.

93. Ad for Texas Guinan's films, as quoted by Shirley, *"Hello Sucker!,"* n.p.

94. Fern Sawyer, as quoted by Jordan, *Cowgirls*, p. 230; comment re cowgirl charm quoted by LeCompte, *Cowgirls of the Rodeo*, p. 115.

97. *Life* magazine, as quoted by Jane Stern and Michael Stern, *Way Out West*, p. 67.

101. Patsy Montana on writing her own songs, interview with author, 1995; radio as housewife's companion from Mary A. Burwack and Robert K. Oermann, *Finding Her Voice: The Saga of Women in Country Music*, p. 84; Patsy Montana on "girl's number" as quoted by Burwack and Oermann, *Finding Her Voice*, p. 88; Patsy Montana lyrics, as quoted by Burwack and Oermann, *Finding Her Voice*, pp. 88–89; Patsy Montana on making a living as quoted by Burwack and Oermann, *Finding Her Voice*, p. 88.

102. Gene Autry heroine as described by Jenni Calder, *There Must Be a Lone Ranger*, p. 169; Barbara Stanwyck, as quoted by Ella Smith, *Starring Miss Barbara Stanwyck*, pp. 271, 293.

103. Ruth Hall, as quoted by Jon Tuska, *The Filming of the West*, p. 265; Myrna Dell, as quoted by Mike Fitzgerald, "Myrna Dell, the Other Woman," p. 4.

104. "Toby Walker" (Preston Foster) on being beaten in *Annie Oakley*, 1935; "Annie Oakley" (Barbara Stanwyck) on her "pretty" rival in *Annie Oakley*, 1935; government slogan, as quoted by Joyce M. Baker, *Images of Women in Film: The War Years, 1941–1945*, p. 1.

105. Description of Ella Raines' character by Gabby Hayes, *Tall in the Saddle*, 1944; Bette Davis in *All About Eve* as quoted by Axel Madsen, *Stanwyck*, p. 273; western repetition noted in Edward Buscombe, ed., *The BFI Companion to the Western*, p. 25.

109. Irving Berlin, "The Girl That I Marry," in his *Annie Get Your Gun: Vocal Selections*, unpaginated; Drake Smith as foreman, asserting his rights, in *Cattle Queen*, 1951; "Queenie Hart" (Maria Hart), on being better, in *Cattle Queen*, 1951; John Russell as the gambler who respects ladies with revolvers, in *The Dalton Girls*, 1957; "Butch Cassidy" (Howard Petrie) in *The Maverick Queen*, 1956.

113. "The Law Lady," *Lone Ranger* television series.

116. Dale Evans, on her ambition and unexciting proposals as quoted by Burwack and Oermann, *Finding Her Voice*, p. 140; Dale Evans, on her success, in Roy Rogers and Dale Evans, *Happy Trails: Our Life Story*, p. 111; Roy Rogers, on Dale's popularity, as quoted by Georgia Morris and Mark Pollard, *Roy Rogers: King of the Cowboys*, p. 96; Roy Rogers, on friendship, etc., in Rogers and Evans, *Happy Trails*, p. 149.

118. Ruth Roman, "Should a Woman Tell Her Past?," pp. 69–70; Pat Brady, "The Morse Mixup," *The Roy Rogers Show*, 1954–56; "Thanks to Dale!!" from *Dale Evans: Queen of the West* [comic], unpaginated; "Uncle Luke," from Doris Schroeder, *Annie Oakley in Danger at Diablo*, p. 101.

119. Buffalo Belle, from *Blazing West* [comic], unpaginated; insults and praise as quoted by Jack Shadoian, "Yuh Got Pecos! Doggone, Belle, Yuh're as Good as Two Men!," pp. 736, 721.

121. Theme song from *The Dalton Girls*, 1957; Barbara Stanwyck, as quoted by Madsen, *Stanwyck*, p. 336.

122. Hallie Crawford Stillwell, biography files, National Cowgirl Hall of Fame; Jonnie Jonckowski, interview with the author, 1995; Delores Noreen, interview with the author, 1995; Georgie Sicking, "Just Thinking: Autobiography of Georgie Connell Sicking," p. 5.

The dreamy-eyed Miss Jennie Metcalf is sometimes said to have been an outlaw. *Western History Collections, University of Oklahoma Library*

REFERENCES

REAL COWBOY GIRLS

Alexander, Ruth Ann. "South Dakota Women Writers and the Blooming of the Pioneer Heroine, 1922–39." *South Dakota History* 14 (1984): 281–307.

Allen, Martha Mitten. *Traveling West: 19th Century Women on the Overland Routes*. El Paso: Texas Western Press, 1987.

Armitage, Shelley. "Rawhide Heroines: The Evolution of the Cowgirl and the Myth of America." In *The American Self: Myth, Ideology, and Popular Culture*, edited by Sam B. Girgus, 166–81. Albuquerque: University of New Mexico Press, 1981.

Armitage, Susan, and Elizabeth Jameson, eds. *The Women's West*. Norman: University of Oklahoma Press, 1987.

Banner, Lois W. *American Beauty*. New York: Alfred A. Knopf, 1983.

Banta, Martha. *Imaging American Women: Idea and Ideals in Cultural History*. New York: Columbia University Press, 1987.

Bauman, Paula M. "Single Women Homesteaders in Wyoming, 1880–1930." *Annals of Wyoming* 58 (1986): 39–49.

Bourget, Paul. *Outre-mer: notes sur l'Amérique*. Paris: Alphonse Lemerre, 1895.

Brado, Edward. *Cattle Kingdom: Early Ranching in Alberta*. Vancouver: Douglas and McIntyre, 1984.

Brown, Dee. *The Gentle Tamers: Women of the Old Wild West*. Lincoln: University of Nebraska Press, 1981 [1958].

Cameron, Evelyn J. "The 'Cowgirl' in Montana." *Country Life*, 6 June 1914, 829–32.

Cleaveland, Agnes Morley. *No Life for a Lady*. Lincoln: University of Nebraska Press, 1977 [1941].

"Cowboy Jo Was a Woman." *Denver Rocky Mountain News*, 13 March 1904, magazine section.

Crawford, Ann Fears, and Crystal Sasse Ragsdale. *Women in Texas: Their Lives, Their Experiences, Their Accomplishments*. Austin: State House, 1992.

"A Daring Western Woman [Fanny Seabride]." *Denver Times*, 17 Feb. 1901.

Dunae, Patrick A., ed. *Ranchers' Legacy: Alberta Essays by Lewis G. Thomas*. Edmonton: University of Alberta Press, 1986.

Dyer, Alvin E., ed. *The Cattle Queen of Montana*. Spokane: Dyer, 1914.

Fischer, Christiane, ed. *Let Them Speak for Themselves: Women in the American West 1849–1900*. Hamden, Conn.: Archon, 1977.

Furman, Necah Stewart. *Caroline Lockhart: Her Life and Legacy*. Seattle: University of Washington Press, 1994.

Guerin, Mrs. E. J. *Mountain Charley or the Adventures of Mrs. E. J. Guerin Who Was Thirteen Years in Male Attire*, edited by Fred W. Mazzulla and William Kostka. Norman: University of Oklahoma Press, 1968 [1861].

Hallgarth, Susan A. "Women Settlers on the Frontier: Unwed, Unreluctant, Unrepentant." *Women's Studies Quarterly* 3/4 (1989): 23–34.

Helvenston, Sally I. "Ornament or Instrument? Proper Roles for Women on the Kansas Frontier." *Kansas Quarterly* 18, no. 3 (1986): 35–49.

Hopkins, Monica. *Letters from a Lady Rancher*. Halifax: Goodread Biographies, 1983.

Hufsmith, George W. *The Wyoming Lynching of Cattle Kate, 1889*. Glendo, Wyo.: High Plains, 1993.

Hunter, J. Marvin, ed. *The Trail Drivers of Texas*. New York: Argosy-Antiquarian, 1963.

Jackson, Jack. *Los Mesteños: Spanish Ranching in Texas, 1721–1821*. College Station: Texas A & M University Press, 1986.

Jensen, Billie Barnes. " 'In the Weird and Wooly West': Anti-Suffrage Women, Gender Issues, and Woman Suffrage in the West." *Journal of the West* 32 (1993): 41–51.

Jordan, Teresa. *Cowgirls: Women of the American West*. Lincoln: University of Nebraska Press, 1992.

Jordan, Terry G. *Trails to Texas: Southern Roots of Western Cattle Ranching*. Lincoln: University of Nebraska Press, 1981.

Kane, Mary Ann. "Woman Rancher, Alleged Rustler, Dead." *Denver Post*, 20 Aug. 1956.

King, Evelyn. *The Range Livestock Industry through Women's Eyes.* College Station: Texas A & M University Press, 1978.

———. *Women on the Cattle Trail and in the Roundup.* N.p.: Privately published, 1983.

Lee, Katie. *Ten Thousand Goddam Cattle.* Flagstaff: Northland, 1976.

Lomax, John A. *Songs of the Cattle Trail and Cow Camp.* New York: Duell, Sloan and Pearce, 1950.

Lucey, Donna M. *Photographing Montana 1894–1928: The Life and Work of Evelyn Cameron.* New York: Alfred A. Knopf, 1990.

McGowan, Don C. *Grassland Settlers: The Swift Current Region During the Era of the Ranching Frontier.* Regina: Canadian Plains Research Centre, 1975.

Maret, Elizabeth. *Women of the Range: Women's Role in the Texas Beef Cattle Industry.* College Station: Texas A & M University Press, 1993.

Martin, Patricia Preciado. *Songs My Mother Sang to Me: An Oral History of Mexican-American women.* Tucson: University of Arizona Press, 1992.

Matsuda, Mari J. "The West and the Legal Status of Women: Explanations of Frontier Feminism." *Journal of the West* 24 (1985): 47–56.

Myres, Sandra L. *Westering Women and the Frontier Experience 1800–1915.* Albuquerque: University of New Mexico Press, 1982.

Neil, Catherine. "Recollections of a Sheep Herder's Bride." Parts 1–4. *Alberta History* 35, no. 2 (1987): 18–24; no. 3 (1987): 20–28; no. 4 (1987): 22–29; and 36, no. 1 (1988): 19–26.

O'Neill, Moira. "A Lady's Life on a Ranche." *Blackwood's Edinburgh Magazine,* Jan. 1878.

Petrik, Paula. "If She Be Content: The Development of Montana Divorce Law, 1865–1907." *Western Historical Quarterly* 18 (1987): 261–91.

Riley, Glenda. *The Female Frontier: A Comparative View of Women on the Prairie and the Plains.* Lawrence: University Press of Kansas, 1988.

Roach, Joyce Gibson. *The Cowgirls.* N.p.: University of North Texas Press, 1990 [1977].

Schlissel, Lillian. "Frontier Families: Crisis in Ideology." In *The American Self: Myth, Ideology, and Popular Culture,* edited by Sam B. Girgas, 155–65. Albuquerque: University of New Mexico Press, 1981.

———. *Women's Diaries of the Westward Journey,* 2nd ed. New York: Schocken, 1992.

Schlissel, Lillian, Vicki L. Ruiz, and Janice Monk, eds. *Western Women: Their Land, Their Lives.* Albuquerque: University of New Mexico Press, 1988.

Shelton, Emily Jones. "Lizzie E. Johnson: A Cattle Queen of Texas." *Southwestern Historical Quarterly* 50 (1947): 349–66.

Sloan, Dorothy. *Women in the Cattle Country* [catalogue]. Austin: Dorothy Sloan Books, n.d.

Stansell, Christine. "Women on the Great Plains 1865–1890." *Women's Studies* 4 (1976): 87–98.

Steele, Valerie. *Fashion and Eroticism: Ideals of Feminine Beauty from the Victorian Era to the Jazz Age.* New York: Oxford University Press, 1985.

Stewart, Elinore Pruitt. *Letters of a Woman Homesteader.* Lincoln: University of Nebraska Press, 1966 [1914].

Stoeltje, Beverly J. "'A Helpmate for Man Indeed': The Image of the Frontier Woman." *Journal of American Folklore* 88 (1975): 25–41.

Stratton, Joanna L. *Pioneer Women: Voices from the Kansas Frontier.* New York: Simon and Schuster, 1981.

Taylor, T. U. *The Chisholm Trail and Other Routes.* San Antonio: Naylor, 1936.

"Their Honeymoon Trail in 1874." *Frontier Times* 4, no. 6 (1927): 14–15.

Tingling, Marion. "Bloomerism Comes to California." *California History* 61 (1982): 18–25.

Westermeier, Clifford P. *Trailing the Cowboy: His Life and Lore as Told by Frontier Journalists.* Caldwell, Idaho: Caxton, 1955.

Willis, Ann Bassett. "'Queen Ann' of Brown's Park." Parts 1–4. *Colorado Magazine* 29, no. 2 (1952): 81–97; no. 3 (1952): 218–34; no. 4 (1952): 284–98; and 30, no. 1 (1953): 58–76.

Wills, Kathy Lynn, and Virginia Artho. *Cowgirl Legends from the Cowgirl Hall of Fame.* Layton, Utah: Gibbs-Smith, 1995.

Winegarten, Ruthe. *Texas Women: A Pictorial History from Indians to Astronauts.* Austin: Eakin Press, 1985.

"Women Who Have Shown Rare Pluck." *Denver Post,* 8 Sept. 1901.

LIVING LEGENDS

Banner, Lois W. *American Beauty.* New York: Alfred A. Knopf, 1983.

Banta, Martha. *Imaging American Women: Idea and Ideals in Cultural History.* New York: Columbia University Press, 1987.

Bourget, Paul. *Outre-mer: notes sur l'Amérique.* Paris: Alphonse Lemerre, 1895.

Bulger, Margery A. "American Sportswomen in the 19th Century." *Journal of Popular Culture,* 16, no. 2 (1982): 1–16.

Cheney, Louise. "Lucille Mulhall, Fabulous Cowgirl," *Real West* 12, no. 69 (1969): 13–15, 58–59, 73.

Christy, Howard Chandler. *The American Girl.* New York: Moffat, Yard, 1906.

Clancy, Foghorn. *My Fifty Years in Rodeo: Living with Cowboys, Horses and Danger.* San Antonio: Naylor, 1952.

Cogan, Frances B. *All-American Girl: The Ideal of Real Womanhood in Mid-Nineteenth Century America.* Athens: University of Georgia Press, 1989.

Collings, Ellsworth, and Alma Miller England. *The 101 Ranch.* Norman: University of Oklahoma Press, 1937.

Davis, Tracy C. "Annie Oakley and Her Ideal Husband of No Importance." In *Critical Theory and Performance,* edited by Janelle G. Reinelt and Joseph R. Roach, 299–312. Ann Arbor: University of Michigan Press, 1992.

———. "Shotgun Wedlock: Annie Oakley's Power Politics in the Wild West." In *Gender in Performance: The Presentation of Difference in the Performing Arts,* edited by Laurence Senelick, 141–57. Hanover: University Press of New England, 1992.

Derry, Kathryn. "Corsets and Broncs: The Wild West Show Cowgirl, 1890–1920." *Colorado Heritage* (summer 1992): 2–16.

Garber, Marjorie. *Vested Interests: Cross-Dressing and Cultural Anxiety.* New York: Routledge, 1992.

Grossman, James R., ed. *The Frontier in American Culture.* Berkeley: University of California Press, 1994.

Jordan, Teresa. *Cowgirls: Women of the American West.* Lincoln: University of Nebraska Press, 1992.

Kramer, Karen. "Bronx Bronco Broad." *The Voice,* 2 June 1992, 136.

LeCompte, Mary Lou. "Cowgirls at the Crossroads: Women in Professional Rodeo, 1885–1922." *Canadian Journal of the History of Sport* 20 (1989): 27–48.

———. *Cowgirls of the Rodeo: Pioneer Professional Athletes.* Urbana: University of Illinois Press, 1993.

Lenskyj, Helen. *Out of Bounds: Women, Sport and Sexuality.* Toronto: Women's Press, 1986.

———. "Physical Activity for Canadian Women, 1890–1930: Media Views." In *From "Fair Sex" to Feminism: Sport and the Socialization of Women in the Industrial and Post-Industrial Eras*, edited by J. A. Mangan and Roberta J. Park. London: Frank Cass, 1987.

Livingstone, Donna. Unpublished biography of Guy Weadick, 1994.

Loeser, Doris, prod. *"I'll Ride That Horse!" Montana Women Bronc Riders.* 27 min. KUSM/Montana Public Television and KBYU/Provo and Salt Lake, Utah, 1994. Videocassette.

McGinnis, Vera. *Rodeo Road: My Life as a Pioneer Cowgirl.* New York: Hastings, 1974.

Mangan, J. A. and Roberta J. Park, eds. *From "Fair Sex" to Feminism: Sport and the Socialization of Women in the Industrial and Post-Industrial Eras.* London: Frank Cass, 1987.

Marvine, Dee. "Fannie Sperry Wowed 'Em at First Calgary Stampede." *American West*, August 1987, 30–36.

Newman, Lajuana. *Ruth Roach Salmon: A Pioneer Cowgirl.* N.p., n.d.

Newton, Esther. "The Myth of the Mannish Lesbian." *Signs: Journal of Women in Culture and Society* 9 (1984): 557–75.

Poole, Peter N. Notes on Women's Participation in Australian Rodeo. Personal correspondence with author, 1994.

Remley, Mary L. "From Sidesaddle to Rodeo." *Journal of the West* 17, no. 3 (1978): 44–52.

Riley, Glenda. "Annie Oakley: Creating the Cowgirl." *Montana: The Magazine of Western History* 45, no. 3 (1995): 32–47.

———. *The Life and Legacy of Annie Oakley.* Norman: University of Oklahoma Press, 1994.

Riske, Milt. *Those Magnificent Cowgirls: A History of the Rodeo Cowgirl.* Cheyenne: Wyoming Publishing, 1983.

Rosa, Joseph G., and Robin May. *Buffalo Bill and His Wild West: A Pictorial Biography.* Lawrence: University of Kansas, 1989.

Russell, Don. *The Lives and Legends of Buffalo Bill.* Norman: University of Oklahoma Press, 1960.

———. *The Wild West.* Fort Worth: Amon Carter Museum of Western Art, 1970.

Sayers, Isabelle S. *Annie Oakley and Buffalo Bill's Wild West.* New York: Dover, 1981.

Shirley, Glenn. *Pawnee Bill: A Biography of Major Gordon W. Lillie.* New Bern, N.C.: Western Publications, 1994.

Sperry Steele, Fanny, and Helen Clark. "A Horse Beneath Me . . . Sometimes." *True West*, Jan.–Feb. 1976, 10–13, 36–37, 45–46.

Stansbury, Kathryn B. *Lucille Mulhall: Her family, Her Life, Her Times.* Mulhall, Okla.: Homestead Heirlooms Publishing, 1992.

Stearns, Rhonda Sedgwick. "Mabel DeLong Strickland Woodward: Cowgirl Wife and Mother." *Sidesaddle* (1992): 27.

Studdy-Clift, Pat. "A Short History of the Lady Bushranger." Unpublished manuscript, 1994.

Terrett, Virginia Rowe. "(Mrs.) Ridin', Ropin', Wranglin' Rodman." *Western Horseman*, 14 Nov. 1949, 22, 46–48.

Vonada, Damaine. "Annie Oakley Was More Than 'A Crack Shot in Petticoats.'" *Smithsonian*, Sept. 1990, 131ff.

Wills, Kathy Lynn, and Virginia Artho. *Cowgirl Legends from the Cowgirl Hall of Fame.* Layton, Utah: Gibbs-Smith, 1995.

Wood-Clark, Sarah. *Beautiful Daring Western Girls: Women of the Wild West Shows.* Cody, Wyo.: Buffalo Bill Historical Center, 1991 [1985].

RHINESTONE COWGIRLS

Books and Articles

Adams, Les, and Buck Rainey. *Shoot-Em-Ups: The Complete Reference Guide to Westerns of the Sound Era.* New Rochelle, N.Y.: Arlington House, 1978.

Baker, Joyce M. *Images of Women in Film: The War Years, 1941–1945.* Ann Arbor, Mich.: UMI Research Press, 1980.

Basinger, Jeanine. *A Woman's View: How Hollywood Spoke to Women, 1930–1960.* New York: Alfred A. Knopf, 1993.

Bella Starr, the Bandit Queen, or the Female Jesse James. Austin: Steck, n.d. [1889].

Berlin, Irving. *Annie Get Your Gun: Vocal Selections.* Milwaukee: Hal Leonard, 1965.

Bourne, Eulalia. *Woman in Levi's.* Flagstaff: University of Arizona Press, 1967.

Braun, Eric. *Doris Day.* London: Weidenfeld and Nicolson, 1991.

Brink, Elizabeth A. "Clothing Calamity Jane: An Exercise in Historical Research." *True West*, Nov. 1990, 20–24.

Brownlow, Kevin. *The War, the West and the Wilderness.* New York: Alfred A. Knopf, 1979.

Burwack, Mary A., and Robert K. Oermann. *Finding Her Voice: The Saga of Women in Country Music.* New York: Crown, 1993.

———. "Patsy Montana and the Development of the Cowgirl Image." *Journal of Country Music* 8, no. 3 (1981): 18–32.

Buscombe, Edward, ed. *The BFI Companion to the Western.* New York: DaCapo, 1988.

Calder, Jenni. *There Must Be a Lone Ranger.* London: Hamish Hamilton, 1974.

Crandall, Judy. *Cowgirls: Early Images and Collectibles.* Atglen, Penn.: Schiffer, 1994.

Douglas, Susan J. *Where the Girls Are: Growing Up Female With the Mass Media.* New York: Time Books, 1992.

Fenin, George N., and William K. Everson. *The Western: From Silents to the Seventies.* New York: Grassman, 1973.

Ferris, Lesley. *Acting Women: Images of Women in*

Theatre. Washington Square: New York University Press, 1989.

Fitzgerald, Mike. "Myrna Dell, the Other Woman." *Western Clippings,* Nov. 1995, 4.

Garfield, Brian. *Western Films: A Complete Guide.* New York: Rawson Associates, 1982.

Hardy, Phil, ed. *The Western.* London: Aurum, 1991.

Haskell, Molly. *From Reverence to Rape: The Treatment of Women in the Movies.* New York: Holt Rinehart, 1974.

Hebdige, Dick. *Subculture: The Meaning of Style.* London: Routledge, 1993.

Heide, Robert, and John Gilm. *Box-Office Buckaroos: The Cowboy Hero from the Wild West Show to the Silver Screen.* New York: Abbeville, 1989.

Histoire du jeans de 1750 à 1994. Paris: Musée de la mode et du costume, 1995.

Irons, Glenwood, ed. *Gender, Language and Myth: Essays on Popular Narrative.* Toronto: University of Toronto Press, 1992.

Jackson, Ronald. *Classic TV Westerns: A Pictorial History.* Secaucus, N.J.: Citadel, 1994.

LaLue, Kalton C. *Winners of the West: The Sagebrush Heroes of the Silent Screen.* New York: A.S. Barnes, 1970.

LeCompte, Mary Lou. *Cowgirls of the Rodeo. Pioneer Professional Athletes.* Urbana: University of Illinois Press, 1993.

McDonald, Archie P., ed. *Shooting Stars: Heroes and Heroines of Western Film.* Bloomington: Indiana University Press, 1975.

McGinnis, Vera. *Rodeo Road: My Life as a Pioneer Cowgirl.* New York: Hastings, 1974.

Madsen, Axel. *Stanwyck.* New York: HarperCollins, 1994.

Morris, Georgia, and Mark Pollard. *Roy Rogers: King of the Cowboys.* San Francisco: Collins, 1994.

Nachbar, John G. *Focus on the Western.* Englewood, N.J.: Prentice-Hall, 1974.

Oermann, Robert K., and Mary A. Burwack. "Patsy Montana and the Development of the Cowgirl Image." *Journal of Country Music* 8, no. 3 (1981): 18–32.

Quinlan, David. *Wicked Women of the Screen.* New York: St. Martin's Press, 1988.

Rainey, Buck. *The Shoot-Em-Ups Ride Again.*

Metuchen, N.J.: Scarecrow, 1990.

———. *Those Fabulous Serial Heroines: Their Lives and Films.* Waynesville, N.C.: World of Yesterday, 1990.

Riley, Glenda. *The Life and Legacy of Annie Oakley.* Norman: University of Oklahoma Press, 1994.

Roach, Joyce Gibson. *The Cowgirls.* N.p.: University of North Texas Press, 1990 [1977].

Roger, Gertrude Minor. *Lady Rancher.* Vancouver, B.C.: Hancock House, 1979.

Rogers, Roy, and Dale Evans. *Happy Trails: Our Life Story.* New York: Simon and Schuster, 1994.

Roman, Ruth. "Should a Woman Tell Her Past?" *Screenland,* August 1950, 42, 68–70.

Savage, William W., Jr. *The Cowboy Hero: His Image in American History and Culture.* Norman: University of Oklahoma Press, 1985.

Schroeder, Doris. *Annie Oakley in Danger at Diablo.* Racine, Wisc.: Whitman, 1955.

———. *Annie Oakley in the Ghost Town Secret.* Racine, Wis.: Whitman, 1957.

Senelick, Laurence, ed. *Gender in Performance: The Presentation of Difference in the Performing Arts.* Hanover: University Press of New England, 1992.

Shadoian, Jack. "Yuh Got Pecos! Doggone, Belle, Yuh're as Good as Two Men!" *Journal of Popular Culture* 12 (1979): 721–36.

Shipman, Nell. *The Silent Screen and My Talking Heart: An Autobiography.* Boise, Idaho: Boise State University, 1987.

Shirley, Glenn. *Belle Starr and Her Times: The Literature, the Facts, and the Legends.* Norman: University of Oklahoma Press, 1982.

———. *"Hello Sucker!": The Story of Texas Guinan.* Austin: Eakin, 1989.

Sicking, Georgie. "Just Thinking: Autobiography of Georgie Connell Sicking." Unpublished manuscript, National Cowgirl Hall of Fame Archives, 1985.

Smith, Ella. *Starring Miss Barbara Stanwyck.* New York: Crown, 1985.

Smith, Henry Nash. *Virgin Land: The American West as Symbol and Myth.* Cambridge: Harvard University Press, 1950.

Smith, Packy, and Ed Hulse, eds. *Don Miller's Hollywood Corral: A Comprehensive B Western Roundup.* Burbank: Riverwood, 1976.

Sollid, Roberta Beed. *Calamity Jane: A Study in Historical Criticism.* Helena, Mont.: Western Press, 1958.

Stearns, Rhonda Sedgwick. "Mabel DeLong Strickland Woodward: Cowgirl Wife and Mother." *Sidesaddle* (1992): 27.

Stern, Jane, and Michael Stern. *Way Out West.* New York: HarperCollins, 1993.

Stoeltje, Beverly J. "Gender Representations in Performance: The Cowgirl and the Hostess." *Journal of Folklore Research* 25 (1988): 219–41.

Suleiman, Susan Ruben. *Subversive Intent: Gender, Politics and the Avant-Garde.* Cambridge, Mass.: Harvard University Press, 1990.

Tinsley, Jim Bob. *For a Cowboy Has to Sing.* Orlando: University of Central Florida Press, 1991.

Tuska, Jon. *The Filming of the West.* Garden City: Doubleday, 1976.

Walker, Alexander. *Joan Crawford: The Ultimate Star.* London: Weidenfeld and Nicolson, 1983.

Whithorn, Bill, and Doris Whithorn. *Calamity's in Town.* Livingstone, Mont.: privately published, n.d.

Wills, Kathy Lynn, and Virginia Artho. *Cowgirl Legends from the Cowgirl Hall of Fame.* Layton, Utah: Gibbs-Smith, 1995.

Young, Christopher. *The Films of Doris Day.* Secaucus, N.J.: Citadel, 1977.

Comics

Bill West. Meriden, Conn.: Visual Editions, Feb. 1951.

Blazing West. St. Louis: Michel, Nov.-Dec. 1950.

Dale Evans: Queen of the West. New York: Dell, Oct.-Dec. 1956.

The Hawk: Fighting Marshall of the Wild West. New York: St. John, March 1955.

The Texan. New York: St. John, June and Aug. 1950.

Western Crime-Busters. New York: Trojan Magazines, Nov. 1950.

Films and Television Programs

Annie Oakley with Barbara Stanwyck and Preston Foster, RKO Radio Pictures, 1935, rereleased by Turner Home Entertainment, 1993.

Bad Girls with Madelaine Stow, Mary Stuart Masterson,

Even the pooch seems to be having a good time in this gathering of Oklahoma rodeo queens from the 1930s. *National Cowboy Hall of Fame*

Andie MacDowell and Drew Barrymore, 20th Century Fox, 1994.

Bandit Queen with Barbara Britton, Lippert, 1950.

Calamity Jane with Doris Day, Warner Brothers, 1953.

Calamity Jane with Jane Alexander, CBS made-for-TV movie, 1983.

Cat Ballou with Jane Fonda, Columbia, 1965.

Cattle Queen with Maria Hart, Jack Schwartz Productions, 1951.

The Dalton Girls with Merry Anders, Lisa Davis, Penny Edwards and Sue George, Bel-Air, 1957.

The Days of '75 and '76 with Freeda Hartzell Romine as Jane Cassidy (Calamity Jane), Black Hills Film Co., ca. 1915.

Duel in the Sun with Jennifer Jones and Gregory Peck, Selznick Releasing Organization, 1946.

Fighting Pioneers with Rex Bell and Ruth Mix (as Winona, Chief of the Crows), Paramount, 1935.

The Girl of the Golden West with Jeanette MacDonald and Nelson Eddy, MGM, 1938.

Hannie Caulder with Raquel Welch, Tigon British/ Curtwell, 1971.

Hellfire with Marie Windsor, Republic, 1949.

Johnny Guitar with Joan Crawford and Mercedes McCambridge, Republic, 1954.

"The Law Lady," *Lone Ranger* television series, based on a radio play by Ralph Gall, first TV broadcast 1954.

The Maverick Queen with Barbara Stanwyck, Republic, 1956.

"Mississippi Kid," *Annie Oakley* television series, Gail Davis Enterprises, 1993.

Montana Belle with Jane Russell, RKO Radio Pictures, 1952.

Oklahoma Annie with Judy Canova, Queen of the Cowgirls, Republic, 1952.

The Outlaw with Jane Russell, Howard Hughes Productions, 1943.

The Quick and the Dead with Sharon Stone and Gene Hackman, Columbia TriStar, 1995.

Ragtime Cowboy Joe with Johnny Mack Brown and Nell O'Day, Universal, 1940.

The Redhead from Wyoming with Maureen O'Hara (an historical telling of the story of Cattle Kate), Universal, 1953.

"Renegades' Return," *Annie Oakley* television series, Gail Davis Enterprises, 1993.

The Roy Rogers Show, volumes 1–6, 1954–56. (Episodes include "Fighting for Fingerprints," "Fighting Sire," "Mountain Pirates," "Empty Saddles," "Head for Cover," "Paleface Justice," "The Morse Mixup" and "High Stakes.")

Son of Paleface with Bob Hope and Jane Russell, Paramount, 1952.

Tall in the Saddle with John Wayne and Ella Raines, RKO Radio Pictures, 1944.

Water Rustlers with Dorothy Page, Coronado/ Grand National, 1939.

White Squaw with Texas Guinan, Melody Productions, no date.

Woman They Almost Lynched with Audrey Totter and Joan Leslie, Republic, 1953.

I N D E X